A WHOLE NEW BALL GAME

a whole
new
ball
game

steve sloan

BROADMAN PRESS
NASHVILLE, TENNESSEE

The Scripture quotations in this book marked (TLB) are from
The Living Bible, Paraphrased (Wheaton: Tyndale House
Publishers. Copyright © 1971), and are used by permission.

Library of Congress Catalog Card Number: 75-24737

Dewey Decimal Classification: 248.4

SUBJECT HEADINGS: Christian life/Football coaching

Printed in the United States of America

Dedicated to

BRENDA,

my wife and roommate

CONTENTS

FOREWORD

The first time I met Steve Sloan was at a national conference of the Fellowship of Christian Athletes. I have been to about twenty of these conferences from upper New York state all the way out to Ashland, Oregon. I've met many athletes, but young Steve Sloan got into my heart and life as no one ever had before.

. . . the next time I saw Steve Sloan was during his playing years at the University of Alabama. I had been asked to speak to their FCA. I got to stay at the "Bryant Hilton," known to some few as the athletic dorm at Alabama . . . plush red carpets and beautiful furnishings. Most of all I was impressed with the devotion to Bear Bryant and to his brand of football. Steve introduced me that night as I spoke to almost a hundred young men—athletes from every sport, plus two or three of the coaches. Also present was Jim Goostree, the Alabama trainer who is a dynamic Christian.

. . . several years later Steve had left the Atlanta Falcons and was coaching at Alabama. He and Hank Knight called me and asked me to come down and again speak to the FCA. That night I will remember for years. I gave each young man a small piece of wire and told them that one end was to represent the first time they remember ever hearing about God. The other end was to represent where they found themselves at that moment with God. It was to be a graphic picture of their spiritual pilgrimage.

Steve stood before those men, many of whom he was coaching at the time, and literally cried as he told softly of the influence of Keith Miller's *A Second Touch* in his life. "Now," he said, "I see men as Jesus saw them."

. . . then came that mind-boggling announcement later that Steve Sloan was to be the new head coach at Vanderbilt! I had been advisor to the Vandy FCA for almost six years, and God was doing some marvelous things as our men came to know Him and to share Him with others. Steve came, and I spent two years of lunches almost every Thursday giving him a report of what happened at FCA the night before, of going to the ball games with Brenda and seeing a warm friendship grow between her and my fifteen-year-old Betsy-Brown, of talks and prayers together when a problem would come up facing someone that both of us cared a great deal about.

. . . when Ole Miss called and asked Steve to consider being their head coach, he asked me to pray with him about it. I knew that was his approach to every decision in his life. When he turned down the offer to go to Oxford, I knew it was because he felt that was what God wanted.

Then, Steve Sloan left Vanderbilt to go to Texas Tech. I felt a great sense of personal loss, but I knew one thing for sure—Steve Sloan did what he felt God wanted him to do. That was, and is, enough for me.

Steve Sloan is God's man. He has a lot to say about football and coaching and athletes. Listen to him—he's been there. He also has a lot to say about love and joy and the Bible and prayer and the family and commitment. Listen to him—he's been there.

FRANK HART "POGO" SMITH
Nashville, Tennessee

1 In My Bloodstream

Football is in my bloodstream.

The transfusion occurred over two decades ago when I was a grammar school kid in Cleveland, Tennessee. There I began playing football, the sandlot version. There was no little league in Cleveland at that time.

All through my childhood and youth, I was involved in one sort of sport or another. I particularly enjoyed football, probably because I seemed to have more ability in that area. I never would have made a lineman for more reasons than one. Size usually dictates what position you play.

My first games of football were pretty simple—we would throw the ball up in the air and tackle the boy who was unfortunate enough to catch it! Then, we would choose up sides and play. We would play nearly all day Saturday at somebody's house. Makes you nostalgic, doesn't it?

Finally, in the seventh and eighth grades, we had a touch team. My first experience with "organized football" was when I entered Bradley Central High School as a freshman. That was actually the first time I had ever worn pads, I guess. A young fellow who thinks that he has to have nine years of organized experience before he can play football is badly mistaken. But what he must have is an all-out commitment to succeed in the game, no matter the discouragements.

As I entered the University of Alabama, it seemed that I had one overpowering desire—and that was to someday become a football coach. I set my sights on it. Frankly,

11

as far back as I can remember, I have wanted a career in coaching. I suppose that speaks well of the positive "vibrations" my football coaches gave me while I was coming up.

I really didn't understand all the pressures my high school coaches had on them, but I did know something of the agony, especially when they lost. Fortunately, my coaches both in high school and college didn't lose too much. We had winning teams.

When I signed with the Atlanta Falcons, I was torn in two directions. Coach Paul Bryant (they call him "Bear") had told me that I could become a grad assistant at Alabama. That was one of the most difficult decisions I had to make—until I was confronted with the move from Vanderbilt to Texas Tech.

So, I decided to join the Falcons. I played with them two years—1966 and 1967. My career was cut short by a shoulder injury my last year. I didn't play very much, but I did learn a lot of football. I was disappointed about the shoulder injury. But my ultimate dreams were becoming realizable far earlier than I had imagined.

I was both honored and excited when Coach Bryant offered me a job at Alabama. I realize how lucky I was to get into college coaching, and I've always been thankful that Coach Bryant gave me the opportunity. I coached there for three years.

In 1971, I was assistant head coach and offensive coordinator for Florida State University. A particular joy was to work with quarterback Gary Huff, then one of the greatest passers in college football.

In 1972, I moved to Georgia Tech as offensive coach. There I was fortunate to work with Eddie McAshan, our starting quarterback. Also, that year Jim Stevens did an outstanding job at quarterback in the Liberty Bowl. He was named the game's "most valuable player" as he threw three touchdown passes.

These experiences at different universities helped me to be considered for the head coaching job at Vanderbilt. When they did offer me the job, I enthusiastically accepted.

I had been advised both ways on the Vanderbilt position. Curiously enough, most people had advised me not to take the job. I felt strongly, however, that this was a good opportunity. First of all, I was from Tennessee, and I felt that would help in recruiting. More important than that was the fact that Vanderbilt was in the Southeastern Conference and was a great academic school.

No doubt there were those who thought Steve Sloan had made a mistake. Our first year at Vandy, 1973, we had a 5-6 record. It was nothing to brag about, but it was a good improvement over the previous seasons.

There were many factors that contributed to our improvement in 1974—none more important than the fact that we had a team full of players who worked to win. The players were willing to do whatever it took to gain respect. They did that and more.

The 1974 team had the best record at Vanderbilt in nineteen years. We finished the regular season with a 7-3-1 record. Probably the highlight of the year was the 24-10 win over Florida. We played very well against Tennessee and finished with a 21-21 tie. Another big win for the team was the 24-14 victory over Ole Miss (the University of Mississippi)—the first win over them in twenty-three years.

We were invited to the Peach Bowl in Atlanta. Our opponents were the Texas Tech Red Raiders. Their coach was Jim Carlen, a man of coaching prowess and also spiritual depth. It was a tough defensive game. Several times during the game it looked like one team would pull away, but it never happened. We concluded the game with a 6-6 tie. The bowl officials awarded trophies to both universities.

Reflecting on the Peach Bowl of December 29, 1974, I have a strange feeling. Little did I realize that the very team we played that night I would now be coaching.

Texas Tech is a little different situation from Vanderbilt. Tech has won more games in the past ten years, and of course this tradition is expected to continue. Actually, as a coach, you are not expected to lose, regardless of the past tradition.

All college football coaches, both head and assistant, work under considerable pressure. But in our competitive society, most jobs are filled with pressure. An added pressure in athletics is that you can read about your success or failure in the paper every day.

Now, I never have agreed that "nice guys finish last." Many of the nicest guys I have ever known are habitual winners. At the same time they are sensitive human beings. They love people. They care for their players and staff members. But they win. I am not insulted if anybody wants to think of me as "a nice guy." I do agree, however, that the nice guy who doesn't work finishes last.

To follow in the footsteps of a winning tradition, though, does not make a head coach's job easier. Far from it. It makes the already demanding task tougher. And it puts on added pressure to continue winning. This is a challenge to the entire staff.

Football is a great part of my life, as well as all the coaches, but I have always felt that a person's first objective was to "seek first the kingdom of God."

> But seek ye first the kingdom of God, and his righteousness; and all these things shall be added unto you.[1]

This is my highest priority goal and objective for my

existence. After that comes my family. Then, my job in coaching.

My job is my calling. I heard a preacher remark, "If God has called you to preach, don't stoop to be a king!" And basically I feel this way about any job. Every job for a Christian is a calling of God. That's why I enjoy coaching and understand the work commitment involved.

When a person comes into a real relationship with God, in depth, it adds a dimension to his life. Then, a man has an amazing freedom to experience and learn and *be*. I agree with Blaise Pascal that there is a vacuum in man that only God can fill.

God is great, infinite, tremendous. And I believe that no person can be truly great without him. Without the dimension of God in a man, that man cannot be a whole person.

As an objective, I want to be a total person—not one-sided, not lop-sided. I pray that God will never allow me to be shallow and insipid. I want to experience God in totality and wholeness. I want genuine kindness, love, and compassion.

There are probably a few skeptics who will remark, "Listen to Steve talk. What's this about being called to coach? Why, Vanderbilt and Texas Tech called him."

Here is where commitments vary. Taking it from a theoretical standpoint—if there is a God, and if he is in control of the universe, and if he created us in his image, and if he has a plan for every life, then it follows that the person who commits himself can discover his place in the overall plan.

God calls everybody that is a Christian. God calls people from all walks of life to do his bidding. If God calls you to be a housewife or an executive or a mechanic, do what he has called you to do.

Perhaps there are those who have remarked, "Steve has itching feet. He likes to move around." I have moved around a lot, but I have felt this was right in the light of what I believe. My immediate objective is to do the best job I can.

Many people in the coaching profession have said to me, "I want to leave my college and go to another one. I want to move to a bigger school—more money, more prestige, better players." My feeling is—and it's from the heart—you do a good job where you are at whatever you're doing. People will begin to recognize you. They will seek you out.

If you are always looking for something else, you will not do your best where you are, because you are distracted. Your concentration will be divided, and you will always be looking beyond the fence to another pasture which seems greener. Do a superlative work where you are, and let the future take care of itself.

What are our goals at Texas Tech? There are two main accomplishments for the Raiders to reach. One is to win the Southwest Conference championship. The other is to play every game as hard as we can.

Why another book? That's a legitimate question. Without apologies, I want this book to help someone find more meaning and fulfillment as they move toward a greater commitment. I would want us all to feel more important. People do rate, no matter who they are. They are pivotal to God Almighty.

It is my hope that the reader will gain encouragement from this book. No person has to continue life in constant alienation, frustration, defeat.

Perhaps the Christian will experience Christian depth by sharing with me in my own struggles, my own pilgrimages. This is why I desire to share a few experiences that have helped me to grow more in depth.

If one person learns to love as God loves, to love as Christ loves, then this book is more than worthwhile.

———

1. Matthew 6:33

2 Friendly Persuasion

John Donne declared, "No man is an island." Shakespeare noted, "I am a part of all I have met."

A person may try to "drop out" and become a hermit, a recluse. But he cannot escape this reality—somewhere other people have touched his life. They have helped to mold him for good or bad.

I am no exception. I could write a ten-volume set of books about those who have influenced my life, who have "brought me safe thus far," to borrow from the hymn. If a person bypasses those who have aided his travel along the road, he has missed the richness of life.

Set aside the bad influences. Every person can remember those who have aroused inferior impulses. Focus on the good influences in your life. Dwell on the people who have meant the most to you and your development.

The men and women who have enriched me are legion. They range widely from the standpoint of occupation and background. They have differing personalities. All have made indelible impressions on the tables of my heart. They have contributed to my life, my growth, my outlook as a human being.

It is self-evident that my parents had a vital and a signal influence on my life. A person has the proverbial two strikes against him without strong support from his mother and father.

A few people rise above detrimental upbringing and bad home life, but bad environment is something that has to be overcome.

My parents instilled in me emotions, qualities, and thoughts that I live by everyday.

My mother is a strong person. She has a firm will. Because of these attributes, she has bequeathed certain gifts to me. Among them is the strength to achieve goals and objectives.

There is a grace about Mother, but it is a grace blended with determination—even tenacity. At the same time, she is exceedingly compassionate, kind, and tender.

Dad pointed me in the direction of athletics. He had played football, basketball, and baseball in high school. He probably was not able to continue a career in sports because of his entry into the Air Force during World War II.

I had abilities in athletics, but Dad served as a "catalyst" to bring them out. Dad's influence encouraged and inspired me in the area of sports.

Across America there are thousands of young people who are not engaged in sports—and never will—because they have received no encouragement from parents and other adults. Talent often requires a spark from another person. We might never have heard of Elvis Presley were it not for a man named Colonel Tom Parker.

Of course, I am not suggesting that parents should coerce their children into sports. This can prove harmful. Parents should gently encourage—use friendly persuasion. This my Dad did with me. And I am eternally grateful that he did.

He came to all of my games in high school and college, often at tremendous inconveniences and expense. He also attended many of my games when I was a quarterback with the Atlanta Falcons. Since I became a head coach in 1973 at Vanderbilt, he has done his best to be at my games. He has been my most loyal supporter, along with a friend of his, D. W. Hogan.

If you are reading this as a parent, stop in your tracks. Several years ago, there was a Tex Ritter song, "Take Him Fishin'." Take your children fishing. Go to the park with them. Sit and talk. Play games with them. Throw ball with them. You're busy, sure. But make the time. Years from now, you will be thankful that you did!

My boys, Clay and Jonathan, may or may not become athletes. But I certainly try to spend enough time with them. A parent who is too busy for his kids is just plain too busy.

Brenda, my wife and roommate, has a beautiful influence on me. We have both tried to mature and grow as individuals and as a couple. Brenda's understanding and love have helped me to understand myself. She has not only been a total wife, but also a total friend.

Brenda's calmness and steadiness are apparent. She is a stabilizing force in our home. She is consistent in remaining calm during the crisis situations. I have had to make some tough decisions about different jobs—the toughest was to leave Vanderbilt. In every case Brenda supplied needed input, but never tried to influence one way or the other.

Brenda is understanding. It must be a miserable existence to have a wife who neither appreciates nor understands her husband's work. Brenda is willing to put up with my long hours of being away from home. My absences, of course, are more frequent during recruiting, spring practice, and during the season.

Brenda is so understanding I often sit back in sheer amazement. Her insights are rare. She can read my thoughts like a book. I am prejudiced, but Brenda is to me everything that a wife ought to be.

How could I forget Rev. David Walker, a friend since

my high school days at Cleveland, Tennessee. At the time he was pastor of the First Baptist Church there, but is now in full-time evangelism. Preacher Walker has raised spiritual signposts in my life. He has counseled with me, prayed with me, and played many a hole of golf with me. Golfers can stand ample quantities of both counsel and prayer!

Coach Paul (Bear) Bryant, the "winningest" active coach in the nation, has had a vivid influence on my life. He is considered by many people to be the greatest coach of all time.

There is not a coach in the business who is so totally committed and wrapped up in what he is doing. Coach Bryant has served as an example of the ultimate in coaching expertise. He is a winner from the word "go." He is a master of preparation, both physical and mental. His thoroughness of preparation is almost unbelievable.

Nina Reeves, the director of Methodist youth work in Alabama, has wielded a tremendous influence on my life. She and her friend, Mary Dell Miles, have helped me underline the significance of in-depth commitment to Christ. Those two gracious ladies have directed me away from shallowness into a quest for depth in my spiritual life.

Nina and Mary Dell have impressed me with their love for everybody, especially for the students to whom they minister.

Mrs. Robert Watt of Atlanta is another person who has been an unusual and wonderful friend. She is the aunt of Pat Hodgson who played his college ball with the University of Georgia. Pat and I coached together at Florida State—he now coaches at Georgia.

Mrs. Watt has an amazing love for young people. She counsels them about their problems. You can carry anthing to her, and she understands. I would advise—and I know advice is cheap—every person, young, old, or in-between, to have one friend with a listening ear. A friend who will keep confidences and bolster your life. Mrs. Watt has been this type of friend to me and countless other people.

Paul Crane and I were close friends and roommates at Alabama. We were close on the field, too, because he was the offensive center and snapped the ball to me. Paul was a concensus All-American center in 1965. He played professional football with the New York Jets for eight years. We complemented each other well in school. It's a good idea for roomies to do that. I doubt if two roommates could have enjoyed rooming together more than we did. Paul and I received a lot of help from Mr. and Mrs. Leonard Culp of Tuscaloosa, Alabama.

Steve Gibson of Cleveland, Tennessee, comes to mind as being one of the giants of influence in my life. Steve now works at C. C. Card Auto Company in Cleveland. Steve is a brother of Gary Gibson, who served as the academic coordinator at Vanderbilt (and who has continued in that post in order to study for his doctor's degree at Vandy).

My friendship with Steve began in grammar school days. We have kept up a warm, understanding friendship through the years. I can almost understand what David meant when he spoke about "a friend that sticketh closer than a brother."

All of these years, Steve has remained my loyal supporter. Our families have vacationed together a number of times.

I see in Steve, and several of my friends, a quality that is almost indefinable, but it's present. They always want the best for me. I have always wanted the same for them. There is no hint of jealousy in the best kind of friendships.

Possessiveness, and not genuine love or friendship, will pout and think, "I hope he falls flat on his face. I'm sick of that guy getting all of the breaks and doing well." Your true friends rejoice when you succeed and weep when you fail.

I would consider all of our assistant coaches as friends. About two-thirds of the staff came from Vanderbilt to Texas Tech. All of the assistants were given an invitation to move with me to Lubbock. A few had other plans, Gary Gibson among them. All of these men, including those who were already on the Tech staff, are my friends. We are a "team" together. We have common aims and goals. We think alike about our philosophy of football. But I would not want to single out individual coaches at this point. I appreciate all of them and what they personally mean to me.

Bill Wade was a standout quarterback for the Vanderbilt Commodores in the fifties. Before our record of 7-3-1, Vandy had enjoyed one of its best seasons when Bill was quarterback.

Bill has had a profound influence on me since I was a sophomore at Bradley Central in Cleveland, Tennessee. Bill is outspoken for the Lord. He is a man of action and of word. Now serving as a bank vice-president in Nashville, he still is active in the Fellowship of Christian Athletes.

Frank Hart Smith is a treasure of a human being. Unless you are a Baptist, or close to the Fellowship of Christian Athletes, you might not have heard about him. Frank Hart is a worker with the Church Recreation Department of Southern Baptists. He is a natural for the position, because he helps recreate people physically and spiritually. He has contributed rare threads to my tapestry of life.

"Pogo"—nicknamed thusly because he was a close friend of the late Walt Kelly, creator of "Pogo"—epitomizes selflessness. With no recognition, he has given of himself to young people through the years. Pogo is a giver and a "liver."

People like Pogo realize that "the gift without the giver is bare." He gives of himself to serve others without expecting praise or thanks. No ego problem with Pogo. Pogo and those like him give and give and give. And expect nothing in return.

He gives unstintingly of his time, money, and energy to the Fellowship of Christian Athletes at Vanderbilt and in the Nashville area. His contribution to the coaches and players on the '73-'74 Vanderbilt teams could not be measured.

I cannot help admiring a person like that, one who goes about his commitment without constantly tooting his horn and pulling his own chain.

And then Mitch and Sarah Kirkland walk across the "front roads of my mind." I had known them when I was a teen-ager in Tennessee and renewed the friendship when I was in college at the University of Alabama. During college there was many a night Paul Crane and I would drop in on them and "eat them out of house and home."

They were living in Birmingham then, and are now in Montgomery, where Mitch is with the Red Cross. Through the years, when I have played a game or spoken somewhere at night, I have stayed with them. They often insisted on my spending the night, so I would not have to drive all the way back to the campus in the "wee hours of the morning." Mickie and Krista, their attractive daughters, are now married and away from home.

The Kirklands made themselves available because they cared and loved. Their door was always open. They gave of themselves and expected no recompense. An unforgettable part of my life has centered around the Kirklands.

The truest test of God's people is this—what kind of givers are they? Are they committed to other human beings? God's people do not want the best seat in the house. They do not expect a pat on the back, although they would probably appreciate it. They simply want to make life better for you. They don't even call it "helping."

Oftentimes you can make people mad by saying, "Look, I'm going to help you." A few people might retort, "Wait a second, who told you I wanted any help? I'm doing OK." It makes all the difference, though, when you help people and you lend your assistance—but never call it "help."

When I played with the Falcons, I belonged to the First Methodist Church of Decatur, an Atlanta suburb. The pastor was Bevel Jones. Bevel is a loving person, and that love was mirrored in his sermons. Those messages reflected a depth and insight. I reveled in his sermons because I was seeing them lived out in the character of Bevel Jones.

Then there is Loren Young, now a motivational and Christian speaker. Loren now lives right outside of Atlanta and carries the Christian message around the nation. Loren has influenced me for the Master through college, the pros, and now in my coaching career. Until recently Loren served as the Southeastern Director of the Fellowship of Christian Athletes.

Loren is probably the most dynamic speaker I have ever heard—and I have heard an abundance of gifted preachers—W. A. Criswell, R. G. Lee, Wallace Chappell of Nashville, you name them.

Commitment sums up Loren's life. And he can instill this commitment in his listeners. Never can I forget when I was an assistant coach at Georgia Tech. We were somewhat of an underdog as we considered our Saturday game with Michigan State—and we had to play them on their home field at East Lansing.

The night before the game we had a team meeting. Loren Young spoke to the team as only he can do. I think his talk had as much to do with our winning the game as any single talk I've ever heard. His talk seemed to give everyone confidence and courage.

Yes, no man is an island. No man stands alone. All of us are dependent on others. None of us are "self-made" men or women.

In Nashville there is an "inspiration" named Jim Sledge. Jim has been paralyzed for approximately eleven years. Tragedy struck when Jim was helping a friend. Jim fell out of a tree and broke his neck. The injury paralyzed him from the neck down.

Jim and I became fast friends. His courage and his will to press on have been encouragements to me, especially in my tougher times. When I have tended to worry or to sweat, I have thought about Jim and his courage.

Jim Sledge has given me the determination to move forward, to move beyond handicaps, to move beyond hardships—and all of us are going to face them if we live long enough.

When I was a freshman in college, I was sort of homesick and lonesome. Most freshmen are—if they have loved home and their parents. I had very few friends and didn't know many people.

So, I found out about a church with a friendly, warm reputation. That's the kind of reputation every church should have. The church was the Calvary Baptist Church and the pastor was Dr. Alan Watson.

I began to attend the church and found a warmth that helped me adjust to college life. A spiritual vacuum was filled. All around us are men and women who feel lonely, isolated, and hurt. If only they could relate to the peace and redemption of the Cross.

Later on, I began meeting a number of people in the church. The messages of the pastor and the reverence of the church warmed my heart.

A famous personality named Paul stated that he was a "debtor" to many people.

I am debtor both to the Greeks, and to the Barbarians; both to the wise, and to the unwise.[1]

None of the people that I mention here are either Barbarians or unwise—but I am indebted to those people, the Barbarians and the unwise, too!

Wayne Atchison, a fellow member of FCA at the University of Alabama, was a dear friend of mine. During college I received letters from all over the nation. Wayne was literary and had a power of expression. He helped me answer several bushel baskets of correspondence.

Tommy Limbaugh, also a college teammate and now one of our assistants, was and is the same type of friend. It did not matter to Tommy whether I was playing or sitting on the bench, whether I was an All-American or simply "one of the boys."

If I could work throughout eternity, I could never repay my parents, my wife, my friends. I am indebted to my coaches in grammar school and high school. Bill Walker was my basketball coach and he coached us to a state basketball championship.

Thanks to Bill Smith and Harold Hensley, who were my football coaches. My senior year in high school we won a state championship in football and basketball! I could write endlessly concerning those coaches and teachers who cared. Without them—their concern and interest—there is no telling where I would be.

Nothing would solve the ills of this planet like a dose of brotherhood and friendship. There is an interdependence necessary to sustain life. We must either learn to live together, or we will die together.

But this has to start where you are. Is there somebody you can befriend? Now, it is easy to become friends with the handsome, the lovely, the influential, the wealthy. But what about a discouraged boy who is on the road to juvenile delinquency because nobody seems to care? What about a heartsick little girl who has emotional problems? What about the man who lost his job because of poor health? A widow who is being eaten up by loneliness and isolation?

Every person in his right mind wants a friend or friends. Is it fair to expect friendship without yourself first becoming a friend? The wisest man, with the exception of Jesus, observed, "To have friends a man must be friendly."

When the acid test arises, rejoice if you have even one loyal, tried, and true friend. If you have at least one bona fide friend, you are twice blessed. Friends are worth more than all of the riches in the world, including all of the oil lying beneath the sands of Saudi Arabia and Kuwait. There are not many people who would aid you in the middle of the night, are there?

This is why I have felt constrained to thank my friends and to remember them. If I were flat broke, I would still be immeasurably rich because of my friends.

There is The Greatest Friend. With him the door is always open. His hands are always extended to you. He is available. He awaits your visits with him. This friend once remarked:

> Henceforth I call you not servants . . . but I have called you friends.[2]

This friend is one who will stay closer to you than a brother. You can talk with him at any hour of the day or night. No appointment is necessary. You always feel at home with him.

You never have to apologize for breaking in on his schedule. He is never too busy to "give you the time of day," or night, for that matter. You can always be yourself around him. You can let your hair down—and if you don't have any hair, you can just simply relax.

This friend is not always putting on "airs." The fact is, and I mean no lack of respect, this friend is "folks."

This friend wants you to be your best. He wants you to have freedom, within limits, to develop yourself as a person. This friend comes to you and me as he is. So, I can come to him as I am.

This friend is Jesus Christ, the Son of God and Savior of the world. Fanny J. Crosby expresses it:

> What a friend we have in Jesus,
> All our sins and griefs to bear.
> What a privilege to carry
> Everything to God in prayer.

Christ is my Savior—but he is also my friend. This is a fellowship and relationship that is the summum bonum for man. Christ can give you a joy beyond joy. And I make no apologies for that affirmation.

> These things have I spoken unto you, that my joy might remain in you, and that your joy might be full.[3]

Most of my friends were and are giving and loving people. They do not give from a sense of oughtness. They do not give and love in expectation of reward. They have befriended me and others for the sheer joy of serving.

There is nothing more Christlike than giving our devotion. The two strategic words in John 3:16 are "loved" and "gave." God loved, and therefore he gave. To give of yourself, in consecration and devotion, is like God.

I've found a Friend, oh, such a Friend!
He loved me 'ere I knew Him;
He drew me with the cords of love,
And thus He bound me to Him.

And 'round my heart still closely twine
Those cords which naught can sever,
For I am His, and He is mine,
Forever and forever.

—J. G. Small

This actually happened in the Cajun country of Louisiana. Two Cajun women—I will call them Marie and Annette—anxiously awaited word of their husbands who had gone to sea on shrimp boats. A severe storm had developed, and Annette's husband was lost at sea, while Marie's returned home safe.

Marie was a Christian, but Annette was not. Marie was with Annette when the bad news arrived. Annette was overcome with grief, and Marie tried to console her. Marie suggested, "Annette, let's get down on our knees and ask the Lord to touch you." Weeping uncontrollably, Annette agreed and the two of them knelt on the cracked linoleum floor in Annette's kitchen.

As Marie led them in prayer, Annette shouted out, "Oh, he touched me. I know he touched me. God touched me!" When the prayer was finished and the two women were sitting at the table, Marie said, "Annette, while I was praying, God did touch you. But he used me. I touched you *with my hand.*"

I owe an eternal debt to those who have touched my life.

---

1. Romans 1:14
2. John 15:15
3. John 15:11

3 My Philosophy of Coaching

I am Steve Sloan. I am not Coach Bryant. I am not Ara Parseghian. I am not Frank Broyles. I am myself. In my heart there is an abiding respect for these men, and many other outstanding football coaches. But every coach must use his own plan.

Steve Sloan cannot and will not be another person. I think it is a mistake to pattern yourself exactly like another coach. The first requirement in one's philosophy of coaching is to project yourself.

Now, I can understand why fans are always asking me about Coach Bryant. It is only natural that they do, since I was closely identified with him when I played with Alabama. In the minds of the fans, the quarterback of a high-ranking football team is instantly linked with the head coach, whether that is the case or not. In crucial situations, they have seen the quarterback in serious consultation with the head coach on the sidelines.

For three years I served as an assistant with Coach Bryant before moving to Florida State as an assistant coach. Then I was able to be an assistant under Bill Fulcher at Georgia Tech, a school I have always admired.

When people ask me about my connection to Coach Bryant—and later Larry Jones and Bill Fulcher—they seem to think that I would approach coaching like they do. That's not necessarily true, although I owe a large part of my philosophy to all three.

A coach, however, must project himself. And it's not a bad idea for a coach to know who he is—else he will project a fuzzy, blurred image. If you are coaching or thinking about coaching, do not project me, or Coach Bryant, or anybody else. In other areas of life this is advisable. Preachers make a mistake of trying to act like another preacher. There are many of them endeavoring to become carbon copies of Billy Graham, and they'll never do it. There is only one Billy Graham. There is only one Coach Bryant.

Each coach should come across *as he is* to his staff and to each player. If he projects another person, obviously he is not being genuine and sincere. In such a case, the players realize that the coach is not being himself. There is no real communication. There is no point, for instance, for a good-natured type to try coaching like Machiavelli.

What I endeavor to do is to relate to the players what I am in the context of my own personality. This is essentially what Coach Bryant does. He has to my knowledge always done that. And his personality is somewhat different from mine.

Coach Bryant is in the public eye, in the limelight. He is looked up to much like Billy Graham or the Pope would be. It's hard for him to enter a restaurant without being recognized—whether it's in Alabama or New York. People want his autograph. He is one of the most viable personalities in America. He has developed an approach of being a little more withdrawn than I would be.

Coach Bryant encounters a different situation, and this reflects on his attitude. He does have a great love for young people, and tremendous respect for them. They come to realize this. He wants them to learn, but his slant is different from mine. He makes his players want to work hard and to sacrifice—he instills this in them. I try to do the same thing, but in my own way.

As a coach it is my obligation and desire to be concerned

for the players. Many people think college football players are petted and pampered (because those people are looking from the outside in). They tend to focus on "glamor," the All-American teams, scholarships, and the pursuit of the pro draft.

But many fans are not aware of the agony and pain and problems and suffering in college football. Often it is the player who can hurt the longest that has the best chance to win. He can hardly move, but he forces himself. But he will not give up for more reasons than one. Usually, it's a combination of solid reasons. The young man has determination, and he's made a commitment. Also, there is usually heated competition for each position.

There are multi-faceted academic problems. The football player has to maintain a good academic standing. This means staying up long hours, because he comes in late from practice, team meetings, or watching game films. Curfews are usually enforced during football season, whereas that's not true with most of the male students on our campus.

There is pressure from scholastic loads. There is pain from injuries. There is sometimes anxiety over problems in the family. There is hurt over difficulty with a wife or a girl friend. This is why a coach, head or assistant, needs to be concerned about the total development of each player. A player's emotional attitude can certainly affect his play on the field.

Many figure that a coach must be stern, Spartan, and hard-nosed to maintain a football team. I disagree. Ninety-nine per cent of all football players will respond to the right kind of leadership. Most players will respond to example. They will do their best for the coach and staff if they know the coach and staff truly care for them and have their best interests at heart.

Yes, I have had to enforce our team rules a few times in my coaching career. Coaching is much like being a parent. If you have a rule, you have to enforce it, or lose the team discipline. If you tell a man, "Don't do this or that," and he goes ahead and does it, and you do nothing about it, you and the team have taken a step backwards. The same principle applies in rearing children.

This is why I am extremely careful in choosing rules, because we are going to have to live with them. If a player breaks the rules—even if he's the best player on the field— he must suffer the consequences as if he weren't the best player. And every player must be treated equally in discipline.

Once in awhile we do have a problem player on our hands. He is often a guy who's having trouble "getting it all together." We make an effort to help that person through his problems, if we can. We worked too hard recruiting the guy to begin with, and we have spent considerable time and effort in developing him—or trying to develop him. But most of all, he is a person, and we want him to become a complete, well-rounded person.

We will not give up on him without an earnest effort. We want our players to have meaningful lives. We want them to be fulfilled. Of course, some players are easier to work with than others. This is a common fact of life. Some are easier to love, too, but you make an effort to love them all.

When a player poses problems, disciplinary or otherwise, you must do everything you possibly can to help him see his position with the team from where he stands as a person. You keep on trying—but there comes a time, when all else has failed, to say, "Look, this is it. This is all we can do. You shape up, or you're off the team." As a head coach you hope those times are rare.

But a few players will reach the point where they will not be helped. They refuse to cooperate. They can't be helped, and they won't be helped. They may change a year from now or two years from now, but life is short. And we have to go on with "the ball game."

So, every coach will lose a few players who cannot blend in with the unit for the good of all. You have to keep in mind the morale and welfare of the team. If you were to bend the rules to retain a player, it would hurt the rest of the team. Each case and each man are different. You are motivated by an overpowering thought: "I must think of the good of the team, as well as the good of the individual player."

When I came to Tech, we had a few players drop out of the program. They, for the most part, were fifth-year players who chose not to return. That is understandable. Sometimes there are good reasons for a fifth-year player not to return.

We have had a few who were undergraduates leave the team. This happens at every college of any size. Every school has a certain amount of attrition each year. Either those who leave feel they cannot make it, or they marry, or they have too much responsibility, or they are not doing well in school.

People ask me, "How do you gather boys from all over the place and make a winning combination out of them?"

They inquire, "How do you motivate them?" There are no two coaches alike, and you better believe there are no two players alike, either.

Motivation is a considerable percentage of the game. This is high on my list of imperatives in coaching. You can have a wealth of talent—big, speedy linemen, fast, agile backs, you name them—but if you cannot motivate them, you have much less chance to win. You can do fairly well, as a rule, because you have good material. But you can't do your best I would rather have average players who feel football is important and can be motivated than good individual players who aren't interested in the team concept. Talent is not all there is to it.

Coaches like Coach Bryant and the late Vince Lombardi inspired people in their particular manner. They, first of all, exemplify a tremendous desire to win. Coaches who become winners have determined wills. The fact is—I have seen Coach Bryant just simply refuse to lose. We were behind, and he still had faith that we were going to come through—and 99 percent of the time we did. This kind of supreme determination rubs off on the players. Motivation was constantly and positively reinforced.

This drive is infectious. Teams like Alabama under Coach Bryant and the Green Bay Packers under Lombardi had so much will they refused to fold under pressure. Every great coach believes so firmly in his plan for winning that the team believes it, too. Poise under pressure is a reflection of good coaching.

Men like Lombardi and Coach Bryant are characterized by *charisma*. I am not indicating that every successful coach has to have that indefinable something, that magnetism. Some coaches, though, are such strong personalities that they walk into a room, and you can virtually feel them in there, even though you may not have seen them.

As a coach I believe in concerted effort, hard work, in reaching goals. I do not subscribe to the line of least resistance. I never want our players to think there is a "pushover" on our schedule. It's the team with the 0-7 record that has everything to gain and nothing to lose. On a given Saturday they can knock you off. I firmly believe in sacrifice, dedication, commitment above and beyond the norm—above and beyond the call of duty.

A coach must have a fierce, burning drive. He must have that determination to win. One coach quietly talks. Another lectures in a loud voice. One coach may be expressive. Another may not be. But if a coach has mastered motivation, it comes across. Coach Bryant doesn't do a lot of talking—but he talks at the right time and says the right thing.

Does this mean that some coaches *have it* and some don't? I am not sure about that, but I am positive there are coaches who have an air of victory about them. I cannot explain it. Obviously, some people have a knack for winning more than others. Some are able to enter a situation and put their finger on the key to victory. Former Coach Bobby Dodd of Georgia Tech had a special knack for making adjustments that led to victory.

A winning team must have clear-cut goals. It must want to achieve these goals. The coaches must plan how they are going to motivate the players. Preparation, not luck, wins football games.

Before the game, and during the halftime, the head coach and assistant coaches have no magic wands that they wave over the heads of the players. They have no incantations that will assure the team of victory. The coach has no masterful oration that will translate the men into seventh heaven. It's not that dramatic. There are not too many Rockne's left from the standpoint of pep talks.

I always plan for motivation—team motivation, individual motivation. Every coach must be aware that he is responsible for motivating the team—getting them into the peak for the next game, getting them "high," not on drugs, but on an emotional level to win.

I try to be positive. Dr. Peale's books have also captivated me, because his emphasis is on the positives. Who ever heard of a political candidate saying, "Tomorrow we are going to the polls and you are going to elect my opponent."? No—no matter the odds against him, the positive candidate exults, "Tomorrow you are going to elect me to this post. I will serve you well. Thank you in advance for your vote." Or, can you imagine a salesman saying, "You wouldn't really want to buy my product, would you? It's not that good, I don't think."? How many products would that salesman sell?

I admit that many of these positive qualities are instilled in a coach by the training he received as a player and as an assistant coach. Throughout this book, I am attempting to give credit where credit is due.

You already are well aware that I have learned from Coach Bryant. But I also think of Larry Jones of Florida State. He knew a lot about people and had an organizational ability. I like many of his concepts of coaching. Then, there was Bill Fulcher, who built a fellowship and team spirit with the Georgia Tech team. Bill is an excellent coach and a dedicated Christian.

Most of the coaches at Vanderbilt came to Texas Tech. I am fortunate, because these men are excellent coaches and good friends. They agree with the majority of my philosophy of football. They are free to work on their own areas, but we are at least basically agreed. None of them are "yes" men. They feel free to express disagreement, if they disagree.

Suppose, though, that I were the new head coach at a university, and I inherited a brand new staff. I could not select my own. I knew that I had to "live" with them. What would I do? How would I go about welding these coaches into a unit?

To encourage them, I would first of all assume the best about them. They are basically good men and they want a winning team. I would explain to them what is important about my coaching philosophy. Then, I would want to know whether they could work within the framework of my approach to the game. If they couldn't, then I would have to suggest that they seek another position somewhere. Before that, though, we would carry on considerable interchange of ideas. What do the coaches think? How do they approach the game? What are their feelings? We would try to work it out. And try to establish a common philosophy.

At the same time, I do not believe in making a coach something he is not. I would not pour a coach into a vat and intimate, "You've got to be this way, or that way. You've got to coach exactly like this."

My approach is to give the assistant coaches plenty of freedom and room for creativity in their areas. I urge all of the coaches to let their players know that we care about them. To me, if a coach does not care about his players, he ought not to coach. On our teams there is a sense of freedom for each coach to work out the destiny of his own area, whether defensive backs, linemen, what have you.

On the other hand, an autocratic coach can receive a uniform response, because his assistants realize that is what he wants. But it is not always a sincere response. All of the coaches are rubber stamps, to a degree. They all present the same front. There is a weird consistency about their ideas.

Our coaches must be free to project who they are, to share ideas, and even to disagree.

There is an old expression in politics, "The government that governs least governs best." This is applicable to coaching, too. Responsibility and trust are two prime words. As a head coach, you clearly define responsibility. You turn it over to the coaches, all the while cheering them on, and giving them input when you feel it is necessary. But you show trust in them. You do not signal trust if you keep looking over their shoulders. You must give them their assignments and let them go ahead with the job.

Although I touch base with them, and I stay posted, and we have a constant relationship of sharing, they are responsible for their part, and I leave it up to them. Of course, I still have a special interest in the quarterbacks and normally work with them on offense. Most college football coaches are self-starters, and they go about their jobs in a very professional manner.

There are countless parallels between coaching and the contest of life. Like it or not, our Maker intended for us to belong on a team. He is in the business of recruiting us. I love Francis Thompson's "Hound of Heaven." God, if I may put it like this, is the "Hound of Heaven," who seeks man and sniffs him out of his hiding place.

God has his own scouting report through the Holy Spirit. There is an apt saying, "Religion is man seeking God— Christianity is God seeking man." And another: "Religion puts a new coat on the man. Christianity puts a new man in the coat." In those expressions is compressed the wisdom of the ages.

You may accuse me of preaching. If you do, I will plead guilty. Atheists are becoming more adamant and preaching their outright denial of God. The Communists, in spite of so-called detente, are encompassing more of the earth's surface and its people. Every ism you can envision is springing up and crying to possess the hearts of mankind. The recruiters of atheism, Communism, weird cults, and downright crazy beliefs are stalking modern man.

But there arises a coach who wants you on his team. He is no ordinary coach. He speaks with absolute authority, but not madly and irresponsibly. You can fully trust this coach when you sign on with him.

Like a coach should, he cares for his players. He has compassion and concern for them. When they are hurt, he wants to heal them. When they have problems, he wants to counsel with them. They are about to drop out, and ready to quit, but he speaks words of reassurance to them.

This coach commands respect, but not respect out of fear or because of threats. People gravitate to him because they can rely on his promises. He has promised you a place on his team.

His training program is demanding. Numerous players fail to grapple with the demands of that program. Yet, the weights to lift are light, and his uniform allows mobility for the player.

At times his players have difficulty grasping his assignments. They may falter. They may momentarily stumble and trip over the gear around them. But the coach's calm manner urges them to pick themselves up and keep going on their "two a days."

This coach is the ideal. The rigors of preparation are worth it. Ahead of his team is the conference crown of all conference crowns. Victory is in sight, even though it may seem dim and far away.

This coach loves his players, and they are aware of his love, care, concern, and compassion. This coach's assistants are not under a dictatorship. The assistants who are supposed to convey the head coach's message sometimes confuse the signals. They are not committed enough to this coach of all coaches. Nonetheless, the assistants who carry the coach's message relay enough of the message to win the crucial games.

This is an unique coach. He never puts people off of his team, even though they may not carry out their proper assignments. Instead of running interference for the coach's team, sometimes they seem to block better for the opponent and his squad. Teamwork is often lacking—the team members are diverse. They are recruited from all over creation—and that's no exaggeration.

This coach is worthy of *your* allegiance. To play on his team is the most superlative honor of all. Even to sit on the end of the bench is fantastic—or even to dispense towels and carry the water bucket in his name.

This coach is my Lord. And I hope that you belong to his team.

4 Motivation— the Name of the Game

Motivation is the heart of effort and, thus, winning. Books on motivation are on sale everywhere. You could fill a giant catalogue with titles of motivational books— volumes on success, how to motivate, motivational research, and incentives.

One of the incomparable thrills of coaching is to view first-hand what motivation does to players. Take a player who is considered "borderline" or "marginal," who is not playing to his full potential. But get him properly motivated, and he begins to contribute to the team, as well as his personal maturity.

The right use of motivation is what enhances coaching, teaching, the ministry, or business—to see ordinary people turned on and elated over what they are doing.

In class the successful teacher is a motivator. In the church the effective minister is a motivator. This is true, no matter the pursuit. The sales manager who can motivate has a jump in pushing up the sales of the people in his jurisdiction.

I have coached with several coaches, both assistant and head, and generally the best motivators are the most successful coaches. There are countless stories of coaches who have inspired players to move beyond their abilities.

Bill Parcells, who was the defensive coordinator and linebacker coach at Vanderbilt, did an excellent job with all the players, but one in particular, Damon Regan. Bill is very thorough in his coaching and always has good rapport with the players.

43

The first spring we were at Vandy, Damon was on the scout team. We tried him in the offensive line, and we experimented with him at linebacker. He was not doing well, to say the least. We had no idea whether he could play, or even what position he might play.

We finally decided to leave Damon at linebacker. Under Bill's leadership, Damon began to improve. Eventually Damon became an outstanding linebacker. Although he wasn't tall, he was quick, tough, and gave super effort. Bill never gave up, and neither did Damon.

Without Bill's concern, it is doubtful if Damon would have made the grade as quickly as he did. But Damon ran. He lifted weights. *Desire* was his number one word. Damon ended up starting both years we were at Vanderbilt.

The main prerequisite to motivating the players is: the coach must first want to motivate and believe that he can. In the second place, the player must want to excel. Bill and Damon both epitomize the attitude, "I will persist until I succeed."

Coach Rex Dockery was the offensive coordinator at Vanderbilt. He and I were together in high school at Cleveland, Tennessee. At Vanderbilt there was a marginal player named Gene Moshier—marginal at first. I was disappointed with Gene's play, and so was Rex. We expected him to be much better than he was that first spring. I told Rex that I didn't know whether Gene could play. But Rex seemed to believe that he would.

The fall of our last year at Vandy, Gene was the starting guard, since he had played well the last part of his junior year. Rex had believed in Gene and worked hard with him. It was paying off for the team and Gene.

Gene made All Southeastern Conference and was drafted by the Kansas City Chiefs of the American Football League! And received an invitation to play in the Coaches

All-America Game at Lubbock. Rex helped him in every way, but Gene also was willing to work to reach his goals.

There are thousands of young people who laugh at the obstacles. They overcome physical handicaps. Remember Mickey Mantle, the Baseball Hall of Fame outfielder. At the height of his career with the New York Yankees, he had osteomyelitis, a dread bone disease, so badly that the infection and pus oozed clear through his uniform. Yet, through the pain and disappointment, Mantle became one of the greatest home run hitters of all time.

In Christianity there is a reference to "the overcomers." Throughout the Book of Revelation there is mention of those who "overcome"—those who achieve in spite of handicaps and even vile persecution. On every team you will have players who disdain the ordinary.

There was a player at Georgia Tech, Jimmy Robinson. He was small of stature, but big in effort. He is five feet nine inches tall and weighs around 160-165 soaking wet.

Jimmy had a tremendous desire to succeed, and his coach, Bud Casey, recognized this desire and helped Jimmy achieve his goals. In his sophomore year he caught 48 passes for ten touchdowns when I was coaching at Tech in 1972.

He had neither size nor great speed, but his heart was bigger than his body. He surpassed his physical drawbacks because of his desire and Coach Casey's motivation. Jimmy was drafted by the Atlanta Falcons and played in the Coaches All-America Game.

David Lee, one of our quarterbacks at Vandy, was not faring well when we first came to Vanderbilt. He had become second string q. b. behind Fred Fisher. Fred had been our starter when he was not injured. Fred did an outstanding job and led the SEC in total offense in 1973.

In the 1974 season, Fred was injured in the Florida game,

and David came in to replace him. Florida was ranked fifth in the nation when we played them at Dudley Field in Nashville. What a test for David. He played like a pro, as did the entire team. If we had a near-ideal game in '74, it was our 24-10 victory over Florida. Under David's inspired leadership, we completed a highly-satisfying season.

The year before, we really did not think David was first-string material. We had played Fred almost the whole time. Fred had done fantastically well, and it looked as if David might not get to play much in '74. Fred chose to play baseball and miss spring practice.

David came back for spring practice and did better than before. David began to have hopes, but the fall of 1974, I had to level with him. "David, you are still second string and backup to Fred."

Because David had worked ceaselessly, it was difficult to tell him the bad news. He was visibly shaken. We had been using him part of the time, but he had his heart set on playing more. But I normally like to go with one quarterback, if possible.

We won our first two games, and Fred and David played about equal time. When we played against Alabama, David played very little in the game. We lost to my old school, 23-10, but we played very well.

After the 'Bama game, David was even more discouraged. Later he felt "dumb" about his emotions. I had to repeat my position—"David, you are number two." But after David stepped in for Fred in the Florida game, he finished the season as our number one quarterback.

He went on to lead the conference in passing. But Fred, in spite of his hurts, was proud of David. That's the kind of unselfish person Fred is. Suppose, though, that David had pouted and given up? Suppose he had dropped out of the picture? But David, of course, would never have given up because he has extraordinary character and a deep faith. Both players represent the best in attitude on and off the field.

Motivation was the cornerstone of David's success.

Many coaches are aggressive, but pleasant with it. There is nothing worse than mean aggressiveness. Rex Dockery is an aggressive coach, but he uses humor with his players. He enjoys life. He's a happy person, but at the same time, intense.

He's the kind of coach who is always shouting encouragement to his players—in practice or in the game. Rex spices his life and the lives of his players with the humorous touch.

On one occasion he had one of our former players at Vanderbilt come to the practice field in a jeep. The former player was dressed as General Patton. This was before the VMI game and seemed to relax the team. "General Patton's" speech was extremely funny and gave us all a good change of pace.

One of the basic principles of motivation is sincerity. A coach must live his motivation.

The aware coach will use his motivational methods at the right time. He will carefully consider what to say and when to say it.

Generally, it's far better to say nothing at all than to speak to the team without proper planning and preparation. Poor planning can cause negative motivation.

This is so important that a coach perhaps should flip flop his schedule of team meetings. Talk to them on Tuesdays and Thursdays one week. Maybe Mondays and Wednesdays on another week. You need to change your tempo and your timing, being alert for possible gems of motivation that are pertinent at the time.

We have all kinds of skull sessions and practice sessions. But we try to build a fellowship on and off of the field. We have had picnics. We'll go out to the lake and swim. We'll have a barbecue and laugh in a relaxed atmosphere, a different environment from the athletic area.

Coaches will often have the players over. Coach Patterson makes a habit of having his players over to his home. Other coaches have invited their players over for homemade ice cream or a meal. Players and their coach can become better acquainted outside of a structured football experience. The coaches are often a "family away from home."

A vivid example of determination and motivation revolves around our first year at Vanderbilt. We were able to defeat the University of Chattanooga, 14-12, our first game. We played poorly and had planned poorly. Then, Mississippi State beat us 52 to 21, with Rocky Felker, their quarterback, running wild. And next Alabama beat us 44-0. So, we had lost two games by 75 points.

We did plenty of soul-searching. We were not winning—not only that, we were not improving. All due respects, we felt that our personnel was just as good as Mississippi State's. As coaches we agreed that we had to do a better job.

We had a number of team meetings and coaching staff meetings. We planned for the best to happen the remainder of the year.

After the Alabama game, we won three in a row. That was certainly a great improvement. We established better communication, and that led to deeper commitment. To a man, the team worked harder with dedication and sacrifice. We encouraged the players to put those poor performances behind them. We feel now that because of proper planning and motivation, and the team's response, we were able to compete with good teams and appear in the Peach Bowl in 1974.

In motivation you must never lose your enthusiasm. If you do, you become less effective. This is true with a team or an individual player. Everything starts with enthusiasm.

We also feel that praise motivation is the most effective. When a player does something well, he needs to be praised for it. Every person needs and wants praise, whether they admit it or not. A player will work harder to achieve when he feels he's making progress. Praise is often the vehicle which turns average players into great ones.

Each player is an individual and you must gauge the type of motivation which is best for him—and all for one reason—to help him reach his potential and be the best player and person that he can be.

5 Learn the Playbook

In football the playbook is the heart of all your offensive and defensive planning. In the playbook there is a fundamental statement about our offensive and defensive philosophies. All of our total information is contained in this book. We include all of our terminology, pass routes, running plays, as well as all our defensive schemes and alignments.

And we usually have information about discipline and training rules. The playbook includes both our offensive and defensive objectives.

As you can see, it's important that we don't lose any of the books. To make up a playbook requires endless hours of work, alteration, and updating. Think what could happen if another team accidentally found one of our playbooks. They would have our entire numbering system and all our defensive adjustments.

There have been instances where playbooks have been lost, stolen, or even sold. To my knowledge, though, this has never happened with a major college team. In pro ball there is a large fine if you lose your playbook. I believe if one of our players lost his, it would not create joy on our staff, either.

The playbook contains on paper, in diagrams, all of a team's plays. It houses your information and gives you rules by which to operate as an offensive and defensive unit. Without it, you have no foundation from which to teach.

Today, with the modern systems and the refining of

offenses, it is not unusual for a team to have twenty-five to forty basic plays, with any number of variations off of those. So, a team could end up with one or two hundred plays.

Every play will have a slightly different blocking assignment. The plays, of course, have different blocking schemes against different defenses.

When a player prepares to execute a play, he has to consider six primary defenses against which to block. If he is not able to block intelligently, it is a cinch he cannot compete. We often remark, "If you don't know what to do, it's hard to perform to your ability." It is hard to evaluate a person who doesn't know what to do. That's why a player must learn about his assignments, or sit on the bench, or be cut from the team, as in pro ball.

Years ago it was contended that to play football a guy just needed "all brawn and no brain." No more, if that was ever true. Maybe it was in the days of "The Flying Wedge." Today a player must be sharp physically and mentally.

How many average people can remember one hundred or so variations in a matter of seconds and realize what to do? Yet, often the total offensive team is faced with this problem. It can give you a headache to mull over the types of blocks to make and where the backs have to run and where the receivers run on certain coverages. It requires concerted study and reinforced learning and considerable repetition.

Each offensive player must know what to do. The quarterback has to have an overview of the entire offense. He has to know basically what his teammates are to do on every play. You have often seen a quarterback hover over the center, look over his setup, and then motion for one of his backs to move before he calls the signals. It's because the quarterback has remembered the overall assignments of every player, and the back is out of position.

When the team members forget their assignments, or fail to follow through, you have a broken play. Too many of these can ruin a season. You have probably seen a quarterback hit a man in the back with a pass, or try to hand off the ball to a back who forgot his route. Those lapses will kill you. And, of course, the quarterback can go the wrong way and create a poor play.

That is why a mastery of the playbook is imperative.

These are "for instance's." For the running play the quarterback might call in the huddle—"right (which would be the formation) 14-G (the play) on 2" (which would be the snap count). Thus, he calls the formation, the play, and the snap count.

Now, for the pass plays, he will call—for instance—"left, 64 on 2." Or maybe "left, pass 89 on 2." Other formations might be "left tight, right over, or left over."

When I was playing at Alabama we used to call the formations "gee" and "haw." Because, as some of you may know, that's the way you turn mules! "Gee" is right, and "Haw" is left. Later, we had Rosaline for right and Lillian for left. We have uncomplicated matters by simply going with "right" and "left." Or "I right" or "I left," if we are going with the "I formation." We try to keep our terminology in the simplest terms. It's complicated enough without making it moreso.

When a quarterback reaches the center and is ready to begin calling signals, he may notice a change in the defense which seems to indicate a corresponding change in his offensive play. He then calls an "audible." He does this by repeating his snap count first—"2" if that was the number. He will then call out another play to counteract the adjustment of the opposition.

In the huddle he might have indicated "14-G on 2." To check he calls out "2"—then he calls out the number of the new play. This requires mental alertness, timing, and good recognition by the quarterback. Thus, he has called a new play at the line of scrimmage. The opposition does not realize that he has checked, because they have no idea what snap count he gave in the huddle.

Think of the split-second timing this requires. Maybe he sees the opponent's safety moving forward to blitz, and he knows there will be one less defensive back. But the pressure will be on the quarterback. If he had intended to throw a long "dropback" pass, he may check to a flair that will catch the defense napping.

Offensively we study tendencies of our opponents. We study their basic defenses and their variations. What do they employ when the opposition has short yardage? Long yardage? On what downs do they play certain defensive alignments? To which side of the field will they move? Or will it be the hash mark down the middle? What will they do on first down, second down, third down? Third and short? Second and long? Third and long? You name it. We ask it.

Quite a few teams run these possibilities through computers. As yet we are not using computers—but our coaches are doing the computing.

We will ask hundreds of questions on behalf of our defense, too. What plays will our opponents run from certain formations? Which part of the field will they use for certain plays? On what downs do they execute particular plays? Do they have certain tendencies when they throw or run?

You collect every possible bit of data. And you compile your game plan against the opposition. You work against tendencies. You practice all week with the facts in mind.

If, during the game, they change those patterns, then you try to adjust—and you even think ahead for adjustment. If they do thus and so, we will compensate by doing thus and so. The team that adjusts the quickest and best during the game often ends up winning. We do our best to have the team prepared, and the playbook is indispensible.

More importantly there is a playbook of life. It is the Bible, a treasury of inspiration for man. Just as the playbook in football contains everything we need to win, so does the Bible. I make no apologies for reading, studying, and appreciating the Bible.

Winston Churchill declared that no man could call himself educated without a knowledge of the Bible. Wernher Von Braun, founder of the U.S. space program, has repeatedly affirmed his belief in Christ and the Bible as the Word of God. Many of the greatest men in history have loved and revered this playbook. Even if a person does not believe the Bible is an inspired book, he has to admit that it is an unusual book which has influenced the course of history.

One reason I feel that people have shied away from the Bible is because they associate it with a bygone era—because of the "thee's" and "thou's" and "ye's" and "verily's" of the King James Version. The King James was translated in England in 1611, and thus reflects the language of that day. Many of us my age and older have grown up on the King James. We have memorized verses from it. We have lived with it. And it does have picturesque, poetic beauty.

But now I am reading the playbook more and more from modern translations. I especially appreciate *The Living Bible* paraphrased by Kenneth M. Taylor. I also enjoy reading *Good News for Modern Man* or *Today's English Version of the New Testament*. They are in twentieth-century language that is easier to grasp and understand, although they can ruin many an old sermon.

My Bible reading includes a blending of modern translations and the King James Version. Many of the verses in the King James have more appeal to my heart. I have a preference for the King James on such passages as Psalm 23, Romans 8:23ff, and John 3:16ff. The new translations throw additional light on my study of the Bible. I have utilized as many as 26 translations by referring to *The Twenty-six Translations* compilation.

Many of my favorite verses and passages take on new-dimensional meaning. For instance . . .

> And I pray that Christ will be more and more at home in your hearts, living within you as you trust in him. May your roots go down into the soil of God's marvelous love; and may you be able to feel and understand, as all God's children should, how long, how wide, how deep, and how high his love really is; and to experience this love for yourselves, though it is so great that you will never see the end of it or fully know or understand it. And so at last you will be filled up with God himself.[1]

The timelessness of the Bible amazes me. The Bible gives principles that help us face our problems today. Yet, no book in history has been so hated, slandered, and censored. *The Koran* of the Muslims has never been attacked with the vengeance that the Bible has been. Neither have the sacred books of the Hindus, the *Upanishads* and the *Vedas.*

In nearly every age, there are those who attempt to stamp out God's playbook. Hitler burned the Bible and religious books. The Communists confiscate and destroy Bibles. One of the first actions of the North Vietnamese Communists in Saigon was to confiscate Bibles and religious books. There are areas of the world where the Bible is forbidden.

In certain countries it is a crime to either buy or sell a Bible in the marketplace—and that's a fact.

So, we who have the playbook should cherish, guard, and apply it to our lives. When I was a kid in Sunday School, one of the first verses I learned was Philippians 4:13. This is an excellent verse to afford help and strength. It helps me to reach down and give more effort.

> I can do all things through Christ who strengtheneth me.

That verse has sustained me through high school, college, and pro ball. It has encouraged me in my coaching. It has helped me to have extra courage and stamina. To me it has served as God's "adrenalin."

Romans 8:28 is meaningful to me.

> And we know that all things work together for good, to them that love God, to them who are called according to his purpose.

Now read it from *The Living Bible.*

> And we know that all that happens to us is working for our good if we love God and are fitting into his plans.

Many people misquote this verse. They think it goes: "All things work together for good." For the total meaning we need to read the entire sentence. "All things work together for good *to them that love God.*"

The person who loves God has a comforting assurance, even though the "Chicken Little's" around us cry, "The sky is going to fall." The Christian has the sense of playing football for God, working for God, going to school for God, pumping gas for God. God alters our footsteps as the days pass.

Many churches and organizations like the Fellowship of Christian Athletes are working to restore confidence in the Bible on college campuses and in society. But a large percentage of people still have trouble with the Bible. It seems difficult for them to read and hard to understand. Sometimes this is explained by 1 Corinthians 2:14:

> But the man who isn't a Christian can't understand and can't accept these thoughts from God, which the Holy Spirit teaches us. They sound foolish to him, because only those who have the Holy Spirit within them can understand what the Holy Spirit means. Others just can't take it in.[2]

If more of our churches and Sunday School classes were Bible-oriented, we would have progress in the context of the Christian faith. There is nothing wrong with having helps and literature, but the basic textbook should be the Bible.

Possibly families are not reading the Bible enough at home for their children to become familiar with it. A young person who has no familiarity with the Book does not have a well-rounded education. Even if a person is not a Christian, he ought to become conversant with the playbook.

If a person wants to know about God, he ought to read the Bible. W. A. Criswell, in his book *The Scarlet Thread through the Bible*, traces Christ through its pages from Genesis through Revelation. The Bible reveals God.

Many a person has decided not to commit suicide after reading a Gideon Bible in a motel room. Or decided to return home to his wife and family. Or to become the "Prodigal Son" homeward bound.

Only recently I heard Ecomet Burley, All-American nose guard at Texas Tech, give his testimony. He pointed out that someone on campus had gotten out the Bible and shown him what it really means to have Christ in your heart. He received Christ as his Savior from his encounter with the Bible. The Bible helped change Ecomet's life.

As a freshman Ecomet was named the most valuable player in the Sun Bowl. In the Peach Bowl against Vanderbilt (1974), Larry Isaac was the most valuable, but I imagine Ecomet was somewhere close behind.

In 1974—and I have mentioned this before—Vandy came close to a perfect game against Florida. Florida was undefeated at the time. Coach Dockery and the offensive coaches came up with an excellent game plan and selected the right plays from the playbook. It was one of those unusual games where everything seemed to work.

During my career in coaching, I have never seen a plan that worked more effectively. We had a good defensive plan and seemed to have the right defense called at the proper time. When the chips were down, we were able to make the big play.

To me that was my best example of a game plan that worked. And all of the plays were picked from our playbook. Short yardage, medium plays, long yardage. They worked. All we planned seemed to click. We made a few mistakes, but our defense balanced the picture. The defense came up with the big plays against the Wishbone, particularly when we had Florida deep in its territory early in the game. We had an almost ideal defensive and offensive game plan.

The football playbook has the secrets to winning the game. So does God's playbook, the Bible.

So, I would urge you to learn about the Bible. Read it with an open mind. If a person is a Christian and desires to grow and mature, he must feast on the Book. I would suggest that he read the Gospel of John about three times, all the while praying that God will enable him to understand. A person must read for comprehension, too.

The Bible has tremendous practical guidance. Like: "A soft answer turneth away wrath: but grievous words stir up anger." [3] "Do unto others as you would have them do unto you." [4] "Love one another." [5] "Boast not thyself of to morrow." [6] Redeem "the time, because the days are evil." [7] "Work while it is day. The night cometh when no man can work." [8] "Husbands, love your wives as your own bodies." [9] "Children, obey your parents in the Lord." [10]

The Bible cannot become the playbook for your life—until you are willing to come to grips with it. Take it. Read it. Study it. Make it a part of your life.

Learn the playbook.

---

1. Ephesians 3:17-19, TLB
2. TLB
3. Proverbs 15:1
4. Paraphrase of Matthew 7:12
5. John 15:12, 17
6. Proverbs 27:1
7. Ephesians 5:16
8. Adaptation of John 9:4
9. Adaptation of Ephesians 5:25, 28
10. Ephesians 6:1

6 Take the Field

Suppose two teams were on the sidelines? Sixty thousand-plus fans were in the stands. The bands were playing the school fight songs. The cheerleaders were going through their routines. All was in readiness—supposedly. One of the national TV networks was ready for a nationwide telecast.

But suppose one of the teams decided that it would not take the field? Can you imagine the confusion and disappointment, the boos, the jeers, and the general pandemonium?

You may reply, "That's ridiculous. It could never happen." Now, it may not happen in big college football—but it happens every day in the lives of people as they refuse to assume responsibility and as they are afraid to participate in the game of life.

You can have a team ready to play. This may seem awfully evident, but they still have to run out onto the field and engage in the game. You have to decide who is going to receive the ball and who is going to kick off. You have to decide which goals the teams will defend. You have to line up and kick off. Untold multitudes of people, though, are not aware of this as it relates to the cold, hard realities of life.

A football team, no matter how well it has prepared, must translate its preparation into action. All of your emotion, the practices, the staff meetings, the pep talks to the team, the student body rallies—all of these must be translated into action on the playing field.

Before a team takes the field, it should have prepared with thoroughness. How many of us prepare for the arena of life?

We become involved in preparation for next Saturday's game almost as soon as this Saturday's game is over. The first thing we do after a game is to relax, rest, and try to sleep that night, which is sometimes a hit-or-miss situation.

I get up early on Sunday morning and do my TV show, which consists of my comments on yesterday's game, with showing of selected film of the key plays. We emphasize the importance of participation in church services.

The coaches and I meet about 1 o'clock Sunday afternoon and begin grading the players by going through the film of yesterday's game. We study the film with as much depth as we possibly can. We run each play back five or six times in an effort to evaluate each player on every play. We will spend most of the afternoon with the grading and evaluation.

Then, we'll have a meeting with the players. There we will give them their grades and explain why a player had 60 or 70 or 80. Grades above 80 are rare. Each player's grade is based on performance.

Then, we begin making plans for the next game. It is understood that colleges who play each other will exchange game films. The coaches and I will begin evaluating the opposition for next Saturday. It is not unusual for us to watch their game films until very late Sunday night.

We will begin our preparation against their offensive and defensive setups. Early Monday morning we will continue with our planning. We try never to delay the showing of the last game's film until Monday. We want it behind us. From Monday to Saturday we want to concentrate only on the team we'll be playing that week.

On Monday we normally have a short practice in the afternoon. Then, after practice, we go over all alignments, scouting reports, and matters pertaining to the next game. The staff works until late Monday night, as a rule. We continue our staff meetings all day Tuesday until afternoon practice. Then, we pick up our staff planning on Tuesday night.

It is our goal to have a relatively firm game plan by Tuesday's practice with the team. We want to have stable ideas about what we will do against our opponents. In practice we will start simulating what the opposition will do and what we will do in return.

By Tuesday night, when the staff sits down, we want to polish our game plan. We want to nail down exactly what we will do the following Saturday. Anticipation is indispensible at this point. What will we do against their offensive alignments? How will we attack their defense? What will we do against their formation, whether it's Wishbone, Veer, I, or variations? What surprises can we expect them to pull? We must outprepare them.

Our entire emphasis by Wednesday is to prepare for and carry out the "game plan." We will attempt to perfect the game plan at practice sessions on Wednesday and Thursday. I stress "attempt." No team has a totally perfect, foolproof game plan. I wish that we did.

On Friday the team has a short workout in "sweats." We do not want to tire them out, or risk injury, on the eve of the big game. We will re-emphasize the game plan by asking questions about Saturday's opponent. Saturday is the day!

But . . . what if one of the teams refused to take the field? After all of the skull sessions, the contact work, the exhausting meetings into the night, the "honing" of the game plan, the emotional strain, travel to the stadium, suiting up, and the warmup period?

It was around 1928 that President Hoover convened a special meeting in Detroit, the motor capital of the world. He had invited Henry Ford, founder of the motor company, to challenge outstanding young people who had assembled from all over the nation. Ford seldom made public speeches. He stood up to speak, and his "speech" consisted of eight words—that's all. Eight words. "There is no such thing as no chance."

"There is no such thing as no chance." I have always felt that this was the greatest eight-second talk in history. But you have to take the field. You have to act upon it, or there is no chance. Preparation demands execution and action.

The coaching staff must do its share to encourage the players concerning on-the-field play. I carefully—and prayerfully—prepare my talks for the team meetings, keeping in mind that, at the appointed time, we must perform and play the game.

To take the field, in football or school or business or at home, wherever—you have to correlate principle with practice. If you please, practice what you preach. It is never my right to preach commitment if I do not practice it as a coach and as a person.

As coaches we emphasize the positive, and try to eliminate negative statements. Success is built on positive thoughts that lead to positive action and effort. This is what I like about the challenge of living for God. It is positive, not negative. It causes you to take a stand, to commit yourself.

Christianity is not merely a philosophy or a system of theology. It is a walk and a journey and a pilgrimage. You can talk about it as a philosophy, but the philosophy has no meaning until it is seen in flesh-and-blood human life.

Mentally you can attempt to dissect faith. You can memorize it. You can learn the original languages of Greek and Hebrew. But if it's not in your heart—and God doesn't live it through you—it has no genuine meaning for your life.

The Christian life is one of "take the field." It is not steam yourself in the showers. It is not sip water from the bucket on the end of the bench. The Christian life is one of involvement, activism, going after the "Holy Grail."

Living for Christ is not a placid, passive flight from reality. It is not leaning back and waiting for the fiery chariot to carry you away. The Christian life is the warfare of a combatant. The Apostle Paul employed the symbols of battle when he spoke about the new life in Christ.

Paul referred to the shield of faith, the helmet of salvation, the sword of the Spirit, feet shod with "the preparation of the gospel of peace." [1]

Many a Christian might as well sing the hymn with new words: "Like a mighty tortoise moves the church of God."

Of course, it was written: "Like a mighty *army* moves the church of God." That's how it was written, and that's how God wants it lived.

The greatest book in literature, the Bible, is filled with action words, forceful verbs. It is not profuse in adjectives and adverbs. Pivotal words are: "Come," "Go," "Take," "Make disciples" (literally, *Disciple*), "Trust," and "Love."

The role of the Christian is not to "build a sweet little nest somewhere in the West, and let the rest of the world go by." Those who follow the Master cannot lean back and let the rest of the world go by. They must be concerned as the rest of the world goes by.

In the last few years, certain sections of the country have

undergone "black outs," when as many as nine states would be plunged into darkness. They traced these weird "black outs" to the failure of electrical power relay systems.

Is this what happens to our world when God's people fail to let their lights shine? What good is light unless it shines forth? We can hide our lights and make people stumble in the darkness. Or, we can light a candle instead of cursing the darkness.

There is a story in the Book of Judges which speaks volumes.[2] Gideon of the Israelites was trying to throw off the oppression of the Midianites. You may recall the account of how he recruited his band of 300 men, narrowing them down from thousands.

When he had his "detail" completed, he instructed them to light torches and place them under earthen pitchers. They were to sneak up under cover of darkness. When they were in the middle of the Midianite camp, they were to break their pitchers, let out the light, and yell, "The sword of the Lord and of Gideon!"

This they did. They broke the pitchers. They let the lights out. They routed the Midianite army of 120,000. They never would have done it without the contrast of the light against the pitch darkness. Darkness and then light meant victory.

If Gideon and his tiny band of men had thought like most Christians, they would have lived under Midianite domination until doomsday. They let their lights shine. They were active. They charged.

They, too, had to take the field!

---

1. See Ephesians 6:10-18
2. See Judges 6:1-8:35

7 Run the Ball at 'Em

Years ago there was a football principle—"Three yards and a cloud of dust." Back in the thirties, there were a few great passers like Sammy Baugh, Davey O'Brien, and Sid Luckman. But basically the game was run-oriented, as teams overpowered each other by running the ball straight at the opposition.

Then both college and professional teams began to accelerate the forward pass. There were passers like Bobby Layne, Harry Gilmer, Johnny Lujack, Otto Graham, Johnny Unitas, and Norm Van Brocklin.

Forward passing became a science, and many teams passed 60 percent of the time. We did quite a bit of passing at Alabama when I played, but mainly we relied on a sound running game. Alabama now runs the Wishbone and mixes an excellent passing game with it.

What has happened in pro ball is also transpiring in college. To compensate for the effectiveness of the forward pass, teams are going to zone defenses. Many teams will commit seven or eight players to pass coverage to offset a passing team. Thus, more teams have gone to running with only enough passing to keep the defense honest.

You have probably heard this advice a thousand times: "Let's establish our ground game first. If we have a running game, then we can pass to surprise the defense and keep them off balance."

It is rare when you find a top team that passes 35 to 50 times a game. We are in the era of the Veer and the Wishbone, and other variations which depend on quarterback option plays, hand offs, and an occasional pitchout.

To win and win consistently, you have to run the ball straight at 'em. Sometimes you can win a game with finesse, but not often. We have a tremendous chance to win our games if we can do exactly that—control the line of scrimmage by running the ball right at 'em.

Even the triple option, for instance, is running the ball directly at the opposition. I am not even talking about running outside. There are many problems associated with running wide—bad field position, fumbled pitch outs, and often lack of speed. That's the reason many teams have gone to the Wishbone or the Veer or a similar system. It gives you the opportunity to line up and knock people off of the line of scrimmage. It allows you to control the ball, and there are less turnovers. You can have charge of the tempo of the game. Making first downs creates field position—and thus a better chance to win.

Probably sixty percent or more of our successful plays are the ones we run at them. Today you must have execution and good power running. Part of your game plan always has to be: control the ball and eliminate mistakes. Control the situation rather than letting it control you.

We try not to dodge the issues on the field or off. I have always tried to level with our players. I could keep them guessing and operate on suspense. We tell our players right where they stand. We never try to sidestep the matter, although it may hurt a young man to know that he is not on the first team. We try to rarely leave any of the players in "limbo."

If they are second team, we inform them. "This other fellow has done better than you have. We have graded carefully and we never play favorites. You need to work on these points. Don't give up. Here are your strong points, and here are your weaknesses. You will have a chance to start if you work on these areas where you need improvement."

When your team tries to become fancy, they take risks. If you go wide often, you risk fumbling or being intercepted. You can mishandle the ball. You can gear your team in the direction of the finesse, "Fancy Dan" play—then when the time comes to knock them off the line, you may have trouble doing it. We expect all of our players to be able to block and tackle, when called upon. A great team must have total defense and offense.

Football is one of the most proficient teachers in preparing people for the problems of life. When we fail to "run the ball" at our problems, when we sidestep dealing with them, we have solved nothing. We have only worsened the situation.

Procrastination is a major problem. Successful people are those who seize the opportunity. They do not wait, they do not delay. They do not put off matters until tomorrow. They act now, not impetuously but with reason. This is a valuable secret of success, both in football and life.

If you wait, if you default on decisions, your problems will multiply. "Procrastination is the thief of time." Jesus counseled his disciples, "Take no thought for the morrow: sufficient unto the day is the evil thereof." Jesus meant that we should deal with the dilemmas at hand. Prepare for the future, but grapple with the problems you face today.

The writer of Proverbs cautioned, "Boast not thyself of to morrow, for thou knowest not what a day may bring forth." [1] Now is the time. "Now is the accepted time." [2] Today is the most strategic day in your life—everyday. Today is the first day of the rest of your life, the expression goes. Live today as though it were your last.

Once they asked John Wesley what he would do if he

knew he were living his last day. He replied, in essence, "I would live as I always have. I would arise in the morning and have my devotions. I would eat breakfast. I would make my parish visits. I would come in at night and eat my supper. I would have my evening devotions, and I would go to bed with the Lord in my heart. Nothing would change."

So, you have to deal with issues and convictions forthrightly. Our nation's morale is going through the doldrums. We have the highest known crime rate in the world. People are scared to walk on the streets at night, even in our small towns.

Watergate has really opened the eyes of our nation. Our highest officials procrastinated on Watergate. It was pushed under the rug. But dirt has a habit of slithering out from under rugs.

When the scandal came out it was ugly and full-grown. At one time the ideas behind Watergate were little. But these little things have a habit of becoming big. It's the little foxes that spoil the grapes. Our society breaks down when we minimize the little wrongs. We have to face them, or else.

Peter Marshall had a sermon, "Beware of Falling Rocks." We ought to beware of the falling rocks that can avalanche and hit us on the heads. But what about the little pebbles underfoot? We are not expecting them, but they can cause a disastrous fall and either maim us for life—or kill us. Watch out for the little pebbles under your feet.

People are lulled into thinking, "It's OK to tell a 'little white lie.' It's not bad to cheat on your income tax—everybody's doing it." Are they?

Hopefully, our nation can experience a revival, a return to honesty and commitment. By facing the tragedy of

Watergate, we vindicated the due process of law in our country. We must stand as a bastion of righteousness and truth. Nothing can put things right like an application of democracy in action.

It is my hope that we will stand for the Americanism that is left in our land. Our country has many faults, but she is still the best country in the world. But America cannot continue if her people bury their heads in the sand. And fail to run the ball at her problems—whether they are crime, corrupt government, pollution, pornography, or drug traffic. We must wrestle with these problems, or our freedom will be threatened.

Delay or ignoring the challenges do not offer the solution. What we do so often is talk about our problems, whether individually or collectively. We call another convention or meeting. We hear more rhetoric. We are stirred emotionally. But then we do nothing about it. We pass through the motions of dealing with our problems and running the ball at them. But it is not enough to believe that something is wrong. We must do something about it.

James notes, "Be ye doers of the word, and not hearers only, deceiving your own selves." [3] In our country we have known what was wrong, but felt powerless about it. We must admit that something is wrong before we can begin to make things right.

Then, we must profit by our mistakes. That is why I, as an amateur student of history, love to read books about history and historical novels. The most vital service of history is to help us profit from the past.

This is why, when we evaluate our game films, we grade the players. We never ride them, but we stop the film and explain what happened when the other team had a big gain, for instance. We point out the missed tackles, the fumbled balls, the poorly-handled snaps, the missed assignments, and other mistakes that we can correct. Only as we focus on the faults can we correct them.

We make a mistake. We face up to it. We profit from it. We learn from it. Then we pledge ourselves to do better and put it behind us.

All around us today are those who are trying to run from the issues. They can recognize that our country is in a perilous condition. Most of the few allies we have left are losing confidence in the United States and its word. And we are in this position, not only because our leaders sometimes give in, but because thousands, maybe millions of Americans, have become lax in their convictions. Years ago in our section of the country, you could leave all of your doors unlocked and go on vacation. You couldn't do that now.

I have found out that most people who become involved in a project have an interest—almost a vested interest. The majority of people who work with the cancer drive have friends or loved ones who have suffered from the ravages of cancer. They want to help because they feel personally involved. And this is the reason that a person normally will go the second mile for his church or his school—or his country. We can all be proud to be Americans.

If only we could see the future. It is best we cannot, because we might not like it. But we must look at ourselves. It's funny how many alcoholics deny they are alcoholics. The first step for a person in AA, I understand, is to acknowledge, "My name is ＿＿＿＿＿＿＿. I'm an alcoholic."

A person can do nothing about his life until he runs the ball straight at his problems. How can a person become a Christian if he has never acknowledged that he has a definite need?

Self-image is vital to a person. If he has no respect for himself, he will not have the capacity to respect others. This is the trouble with the chronic criminal personality. He has no respect for himself. He feels inadequate. He feels meaningless. He sees no hope. For that reason, he cannot see the value of himself, or others. People with poor self-images back down from problems because they do not feel adequate to handle them. They feel helpless. Rather than deal with anything, they continue to put it off.

We put off our sin problem. We put off straightening out our family situation. We put off making up with our neighbor. We put off going to a person we have offended. We sidestep the problems and do not deal with them.

Horror becomes the result of neglecting cancer. Many people fail to have a biopsy or an X-ray to check for cancer. Sometimes, because of not facing the problem, they end up having an *autopsy*. If you go ahead perhaps they can cut out the cancer or treat it with cobalt—and get rid of it. Nothing ventured, nothing gained.

Run the ball at 'em. Those with success in life have learned to block crisply and to do it now.

> Forgetting the past and looking forward to what lies ahead, I strain to reach the end of the race and receive the prize for which God is calling us up to heaven because of what Christ Jesus did for us.[4]

---

1. Proverbs 27:1
2. 2 Corinthians 6:2
3. James 1:22
4. Philippians 3:13-14

8 Third Down and Clutch Yardage

"Third down and clutch yardage" is a phrase that has increased drastically the use of Rolaids by coaches. Every third down situation is critical and important. Most games are won by the team which makes the most third down conversions.

I could never forget the Alabama-Ole Miss game in 1965. It was my senior year at Alabama, and this was a must game for us. Fortunately, we were able to win, 17-16, in the last seconds.

On our drive for the winning touchdown, he had fourth down three times. Each time we were able to make the first down by inches. This last drive carried 89 yards as time ran out. David Ray's extra point made the difference as he expertly kicked the conversion. (David helped win several games for Alabama in 1964-1965.)

The previous Wednesday, Coach Bryant had conducted an early morning practice on short yardage situations, because we had done poorly in Tuesday's practice. Coach Bryant always seemed to anticipate what type of practice we needed in order to win. After the morning practice, we had a regular Wednesday practice.

I remember that Jerry Duncan caught a "tackle eligible" pass on that series against Ole Miss. Ray Perkins made a fantastic catch for a 30-yard gain. Steve Bowman and Les Kelley made the necessary yardage on fourth down short yardage. Alabama was named the national champion that year, but without those clutch third down conversions, we never would have been national champions.

When I was coaching at Georgia Tech, we had a third down and clutch yardage play against Tulane. Eddie Mc-Ashan, our quarterback, threw a pass to Mike Owen. Mike and Tulane's defensive backs did the rest. The defensive backs bumped into one another, and Mike capitalized on the play by racing 60 yards for the winning t. d. Without that win, we would not have received a bid to the Liberty Bowl. One play on third down and clutch yardage can make or break your team.

Then, I recall another key play which opened the way for a bowl invitation. When I was with Florida State, we were playing South Carolina coached by Paul Dietzel at the time. Early in the game we were not able to move the ball.

Our quarterback was Gary Huff, who is now with the Chicago Bears. We had a third down play, and we were backed up in our own territory. Gary threw a pass to Rhett Dawson. Rhett, who was drafted by the Houston Oilers, made a super catch. That one catch seemed to turn the game around.

At the time South Carolina was leading, but not for long. We ended up winning by a comfortable margin, but that third down play ignited our team. Winning the ball game enabled us to be invited to the Fiesta Bowl. Once again a third down play seemed to mean the difference between a bowl invitation and staying at home.

When I think in terms of personal "third down and clutch yardage" situations, I am nearly always reminded of Jamie O'Rourke at Vanderbilt, who gained over 1,000 yards in 1974, including the Peach Bowl. In 1973 during the early fall practice, he dove over the goal line and injured both of his knees. The knees were operated on, and he had both of them in casts at the same time.

If ever a guy had the odds stacked against him, Jamie

Top: Dr. Grover Murray, president of Texas Tech, introducing me at a basketball game. Bottom: Every coach received a portrait for participating in the Coaches All-America Game. (Texas Tech Photos)

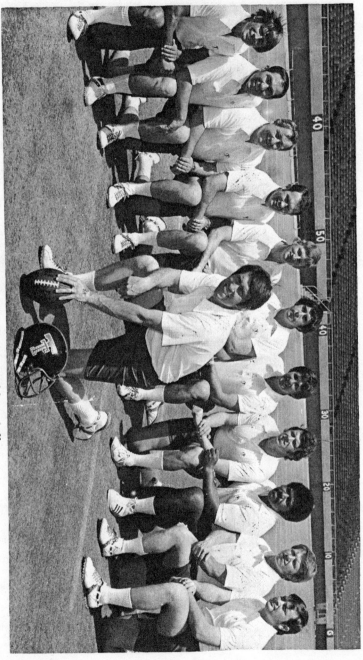

The 1975 Texas Tech coaching staff

Top: Whispering is part of the mystery of football.
Bottom: My favorite way to coach—here I am talking
with Rodney Allison, one of Texas Tech's quarterbacks. (Texas Tech Photos)

Top: The fellow with the hat on—his team won. Bottom: Jim Lampley does the interviews for ABC during televised games. (Texas Tech Photo)

Top: Brenda and I at our home when we lived in Nashville Bottom: Young prospects (left to right) Clay Sloan, Matt MacIntyre, and Jonathan Sloan (1974)

Top: To be a part of the 1975 Coaches All-America Game was a great thrill. Bottom: Spring practice at Texas Tech—tight end Sylvester Brown and I (Texas Tech Photos)

Top: Bill Fulcher, head coach, and I at Georgia Tech (Georgia Tech Photo) Bottom: Coach Battle and I consoled each other after we tied 21-21 in Nashville. (*Tennessean* Photo by Frank Empson)

The Vanderbilt coaching staff—1974 (*Nashville Banner* Photo by Charles Warren)

The official made me do it! (Texas Tech Photo)

The "Section N Gang" is one of Vanderbilt's greatest morale builders and loyal supporters. This picture was taken after Vanderbilt beat Ole Miss in 1974, 24-14. (*Tennessean* Photo by Ray Cobb)

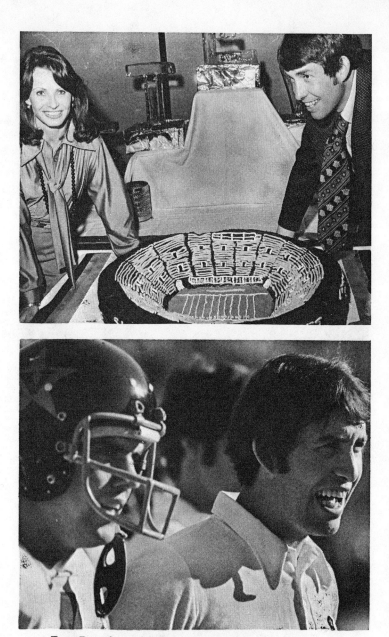

Top: Brenda and I at a recruiting dinner after one of
the Vanderbilt games (*Tennessean* Photo by S. A.
Tarkington) Bottom: David Lee, Vanderbilt team cap-
tain, and I watch the defense—1974. (*News-Free Press*
Photo by Benny Collins)

Top: A cowboy at heart—a hillbilly in reality! Bottom: Coach Dick Crum and I at the All-American Game in Lubbock (Texas Tech Photo)

Grant Teaff was the "Coach of the Year" in 1974, as Baylor won the SWC title. We were the opposing coaches in the 1975 Coaches All-America Game. (Texas Tech Photo)

Vanderbilt's fine quarterback, Fred Fisher—I think I was telling him that the headphones were not working. (Vanderbilt Photo)

Top: Sometimes it's easier to look for lost pocket-books. (Texas Tech Photo) Bottom: Victory—how sweet it is! (Vanderbilt Photo)

Top: Wonder what Plato would do in this situation?
(Texas Tech Photo) Bottom: I hear it! It's "Cattle Call." *(Nashville Banner Photo)*

did. The Flip Pitts family there in Nashville—because they are such wonderful people—took Jamie in and helped to rehabilitate him. Jamie had more than his share of agonizing days. Jamie worked long hours lifting weights and was able to get completely well. Jamie was as tough a football player and a competitor as I have ever known.

In football you have to anticipate those third down and clutch yardage situations. The coaches work tedious hours studying the opposition's third down defenses. What will they do on offense or defense?

They may gravitate to a certain defense, so you come up with a play or plays to run against the expected defense. All is based on careful preparation.

And there is always the intangible factor—what will your team do against adversity? Will it fold or will it rise up and overcome the crises? My first year at Vanderbilt we had trouble meeting the third down emergencies. Everytime the bad occurred, we could expect the worse to follow. We were not able to overcome adversity.

As our players matured and returned the following year, we were "jelling" as a unit. We began to overcome adversity and make good things happen. We might fumble, but our defense would stop their offense. We might throw an interception, but our defense would again stop them.

What makes it all the more intriguing is: you never know in those clutch situations the overall importance of one play. That is, until hindsight becomes operative. A winning season could hinge on one play. A bowl game could rest on one play.

As a college quarterback, I faced more than my share of the third down plays. In life the third downs have centered around my career decisions. As yet I have not suffered severe tragedies, although each family will eventually face them.

My first crucial decision was where to attend college. I received offers from several schools. Alabama was my final choice—I have never regretted it, although perhaps it was not my own choice. I'll explain later.

Then, I confronted the question of where to play pro ball. I had two excellent offers, one from the New York Jets, and the other with the Atlanta Falcons. Joe Namath was with the Jets, and we had played together in college. And Paul Crane, my roommate, had just signed with the Jets. There were two solid reasons for signing with the Jets. But, in the end, I felt the best thing to do was play with Atlanta.

When I hurt my shoulder with the Falcons, I returned to the University of Alabama in January of 1968. I was doing some studying there—I spent most of my time at the library.

One day Coach Bryant sent for me. I was in between jobs at the time. And Coach Bryant wanted me to join his staff as an assistant and coach of the quarterbacks. How lucky can you get? It is not easy to break into college coaching, and to have this opportunity was more than I could have ever asked for. I coached there three years and worked with many fine players, including Scott Hunter, Neb Hayden, and Terry Davis.

The move from Alabama to Florida State, where I became their assistant head coach and offensive coordinator, was a third down decision. So was my move to Georgia Tech as offensive coach.

But my most difficult career decision was leaving Vanderbilt for Texas Tech. The move created considerable discussion in sports circles. On December 29, 1974, Vanderbilt and Texas Tech had played to a tie in the Peach Bowl at Atlanta. We had tied 6-6, and both teams had received winner's trophies. A couple of weeks before,

Coach Carlen had announced that he was accepting a position with South Carolina as head football coach.

Texas Tech, through athletic director J. T. King, had expressed an interest in my coming as head football coach. After the game I flew out to Lubbock and had a conference with the Tech people. I was extremely impressed with Coach King and Texas Tech.

After all, what the Vanderbilt team had accomplished was not done overnight. We had wound up most of our recruiting, and certainly felt good about it. The players were depending on me to stay. There was an indescribably warm fellowship and friendship with them.

Vanderbilt had granted me my first opportunity to serve as a head coach. Athletic director Clay Stapleton had given me the chance, even though I was a young coach. The Vandy fans had been better every game, especially the "Section N Gang." This group had really helped our spirits. My biggest problem in leaving was my relationship with the players.

The fans. The press. My friends. All wanted a definitive answer. Why are you leaving Vanderbilt? Why did you build us up to let us down? I received a number of critical letters, which I may well have deserved. To my knowledge only one Nashville editorial was captiously critical of me. Most of the sportswriters were sympathetic and understanding.

I personally think I deserved some of the criticism. All day long on New Year's Eve, the last day of 1974, I fought with the decision. Texas Tech was in constant touch. The Vanderbilt people were concerned. Would I stay or leave?

After 10 P.M. on December 31, 1974, I announced that I was remaining at Vanderbilt. The news was sent out on radio and television and the early editions of *The Nashville Tennessean* reported that I was staying.

The following day, though, I had no peace. Never before had I changed a major decision already announced. What would the fans think? Would I change the decision and live with the consequences—the criticism, the misunderstanding?

On New Year's Day, 1975, I called J. T. King and asked if Tech would still have me. Mr. King replied, "Yes." With a feeling of embarrassment, I announced to the Vanderbilt officials and the press that I had reconsidered and was leaving for Tech. I had to move. To do otherwise would have been unfair to everybody concerned.

Throughout my life I have tried to do the right, the "best thing to do." And I became convinced that moving to Texas Tech was best for all concerned.

That experience taught me an indelible lesson. If I can help it, I will never make a big decision after 10 P.M. at night. I cannot make that a rule of thumb for others, but I can for myself.

I was tired and emotionally drained. So much was at stake. To err is human—to forgive, divine. I was human. Most of the Vanderbilt people—personnel, fans, and others—were divine in that they forgave. Letters to the Nashville papers were overwhelmingly in sympathy with my decision "if I felt it was the right thing to do."

In all of these decisions I have soul-searchingly prayed for heavenly guidance. You have to weigh all kinds of advantages and disadvantages—salary, TV money, fringe benefits, personnel—but prayer must swing the balance for me. It did in the choice of my college, my pro team, my coaching responsibilities.

Call it pietism, but prayerful decision-making is always the best way. I have made career decisions with which I did not feel agreement at the time—yet it was my firm impression that God wanted certain courses of action. For instance, when I first attended Alabama, I was not sold on the idea—but still I felt it was right. It worked out for the best. God has a way of working things out.

Throughout life I have been constrained to follow the dictates of my heart—as God moves on my heart. If a person wants to flip a coin, that's his business. If he rolls dice, that's his affair. If he writes the pluses on one side and the minuses on the other, more power to him. But I have to base my decisions on a sense of calling.

When a person is following through on his calling, he can live with both the praise and the criticism. In fact, I can even be thankful for the latter. Not all criticism is invalid.

No person is exempt from the third down plays in life. Even the best person—consider Job of the Bible—is prone to problems, heartaches, sorrows. People still die. They become ill. They contract cancer. They have accidents.

But God is there—there to carry us through. He is bigger than our problems. The best third down play of all is having God as your quarterback.

When crises come, and they will come, we can count on Christ to be there to see us through. This is man's greatest resource. The love of God and the strength of God are enough.

Suppose you had to confront eleven men averaging 230 pounds or more—and you had to do it by yourself? It sounds ridiculous from the standpoint of football. One strength about playing on a college team is the thrill of comradeship. In college I was behind an All-American center who snapped the ball. In front of me was a line second to none, tackles, guards, and ends. To my side and behind me were three great backs. I was not alone against the defensive linemen and those blitzing linebackers and the occasional safety.

When the third down arises, it is a comfort to have companions. This is why I appreciate the prayers of my friends. One of my greatest thrills is being able to pray for a friend who is in need. Intercession is a divine ministry.

Are you backed up almost to your end zone? Are the third down plays stifling you? Is the tension jangling your nerves?

Call on your Best Friend, who specializes in dealing with crises.

9 On the Recruiting Trail

How often I have heard Coach Bryant remark, "You don't outcoach people—you outrecruit them."

I think, in the long run, every coach must recognize this basic principle, or face the alumni firing squad. Recruiting is the crux of building a championship football team.

In recent years, with all of the emphasis on winning, the recruiting situation has become even more critical. There is no letup in going after the quality players from high schools and junior colleges.

It's self-evident. Generally the team with the best players has the best chance to win. You can have the most astute coaches in the business—without the players they have less chance to win. What would Eisenhower and MacArthur have done without the troops in World War II? And the best coaches in the business are the first to acknowledge this cold piece of data.

So, you and your staff try to line up all of the talented material that you can sign—and there are limitations on the number of scholarships, thirty in the Southwest Conference. Once in awhile, a walk-on makes it big—even becomes all-conference, but this is somewhat rare.

Recruiting is probably our most vital activity, outside of actually going out onto the field and playing the game. All of the schools with which I have coached—Alabama, Florida State, Georgia Tech, Vanderbilt, and now Texas Tech—have realized the role of recruiting.

It runs in a cycle. You have successful recruiting. You **97** end up establishing yourself as a winner, if all goes as planned. The university builds itself a reputation as a football power. Young men with football abilities are drawn to a winner, especially if they feel there is a place for them. So, there is nothing like successful recruiting to sustain your winning. That begets a tradition conducive to recruiting.

We gear up to recruit the players. We become detailed and highly organized. We can afford to leave no stone unturned—you can overlook no player who has merit. The staff works endless hours at recruiting. Mike Pope, who came here from Florida State University, is our recruiting coordinator. Mike is one of the best I've ever been around. He has excellent rapport with young people, and a good plan.

On our staff we plan for recruiting. We have a yearly plan, but there are certain limitations on what we may do in recruiting. In Texas you cannot contact a player until August 15, right before his senior year in high school. In Tennessee you could go out and talk to players in the spring of their junior year. Every conference, of course, has slightly different regulations and signing dates.

In Texas, though, you cannot sign a player until the first Tuesday in February of a boy's senior year. In the Southeastern Conference you can sign up a boy beginning the second Saturday in December of his senior year. Any deviation from this, naturally, would constitute a serious violation.

In order to recruit in college, we give every coach an area to cover, an area we feel fits his personality and enables him to mix properly with the people. Every coach has an area of the state, and when we go outside the state, we have specific coaches assigned there, too.

We try to make contact on a friendly basis with all of

the coaches in our state, at least most of them. There is a lot of ground to cover in Texas. We have a mailout list, and we send out information about Texas Tech to the coaches.

Our coaches at Tech scout as many high school games as possible. Here in Texas there is a strong junior college program, so we keep close watch on jc players, too. Many players who are not quite ready for major college football go to junior college, mature, and often are ready for university-level competition.

Our coaches have to be pr (public relations) men for our university. They have to contact and meet all types of people. They have to nurture a rapport with coaches, parents, and the boys themselves. They cannot begin to build this relationship, as I mentioned, until August 15, prior to a player's senior year.

A man who knows football but is squeamish about meeting people in every conceivable situation had better forget the business of football coaching. Most successful recruiters have to sell themselves first. The good recruiter is able to sell both himself and his college. He projects the pluses of the college he represents. He must have answers right at the tips of his fingers. A coach has to "have it altogether" as a person who communicates with other people of all ages and personalities.

This is essential, because college recruiting is fierce in its competition. It is not uncommon for ten or more schools to have an extraordinary interest in the same player.

How do we keep up with thousands of football players in the state? Well, that's a good question. We do it by establishing contact with the coaches. We attend many key football games across the state. The alumni often make recommendations. They give us names. They write letters to us and for us. They make phone calls. You look at players on the field. You watch games films. Almost all high schools have films available for you to watch and evaluate.

The great players in high school and junior college are not hard to find. They always stand out. It's the marginal players that can turn into good players that are hard to recognize. It requires a coach with talent to spot the players that are marginal, but who can develop with the proper practice, experience, and seasoning.

This is where your better recruiters can excel. They can spot diamonds in the rough. They can forecast potential. Maybe all of the other colleges will pass up a boy, but one of your coaches reads between the lines.

It requires no special talent to recognize the extraordinary player. But it requires genius to see the latent ability that could blossom into all-conference honors within two or three years.

Let's think about a hypothetical player. He's Mo Stravinsky of the New Rockland High School. How will we go about recruiting him? The coach who is recruiting in that area of the state must have approved him and expressed an interest in him. We then cross check Mo. We gather all the data we can. We watch him on the field. We look at him in game films.

After August 15 before his senior year, we establish contact with him. Sometimes it's in a phone call or letter, but face-to-face contact is the best. We call him or write him from time-to-time after our initial contact. We keep him posted about the university. During his senior year we stay in touch with him. We may drop in on him—we also call and/or write him.

I would become involved in recruiting Mo by telephone at first. Also, we may have alumni in the area visit the boy and his family. We'll have the young man come in and visit our school. We'll again present our program and share our philosophy of football with him. Then, it becomes a matter of touching base with him until the February signing date. Hopefully, Mo will sign a grant-in-aid with us.

After that important date in August, there is no limit to the amount of times we can contact Mo. Tact is important, and I think if a coach camped on Mo's doorstep, he could turn the player off, as well as his parents. A few high schools set limits, too, on the number of contacts we can make.

At Vanderbilt we never sold ourselves short. But we were in the process of building a solid program. When we went there, we felt if a boy had some size and some speed, even though he wasn't a spectacular high school player, he might fit into our plans.

Two of these young men will not mind my mentioning their names. Mike Birdsong whom we recruited for Vandy was not super when we signed him. But he was big, had determination, and will develop into a splendid player. He had good speed, but simply had not matured enough in high school to become a great player.

And there was big Dennis Harrison of Murfreesboro, Tennessee. He was big, could run, but still required maturing. Even though he was six-and-a-half feet tall and large, not every college was interested in him. Yet, he developed and was named the outstanding defensive player in the Peach Bowl when Vanderbilt and Texas Tech tied 6-6. Not many major colleges had offered him scholarships.

Both of these young men came from fine families. That's crucial. If a player's family life is bad, it may mean troubles later on in college. I cannot emphasize too strongly the role of the family to support and sustain any young person.

And you find this, too. Many times the bigger boy in

high school has not matured like the smaller one. The big boys at times tend to be clumsy. Some big boys mature later on in college and become better coordinated—and then actually play to their potential in college or pro ball.

If a coach is recruiting, I would suggest that he sell himself to the player's family. If they dislike the coach, he has already lost out. The coach should be concerned about more than merely signing the boy on the dotted line of the grant-in-aid. He should show genuine concern for the family and what they want for their son. The coach should want to solidify the relationship.

When we recruit—and at all times—we want to present a winsome image of our school. We think it's the best and has the most to offer from every standpoint. I wouldn't be here if I didn't believe that.

We want to be totally honest in our recruiting. We never want to downgrade a competing school. People—at least most people—are able to see through that kind of inferior strategy. All of the schools in our conference are excellent. Nothing is gained by running down your competition.

We stick to the plus factors about our school. We key in on what our school and its program will do to help a young man realize his goals and objectives in life. We level with him about our requirements. We hope to offer him a well-rounded program of academics. We pray that he will like our type of football, our coaches, and the spirit of the school.

My advice to a young football player is: study your books as hard as you play and practice. Many a talented player falls by the wayside because he fails to make it scholastically. You must maintain a 2.0 average to remain on the football team. There are some courses of study which require higher than 2.0 for a person to continue in those courses. If a young man is shaky in his books, it hurts his chances for succeeding as a college football player.

Yes, recruiting is the life's blood of a college football team. There is another recruiting, though, that is far more significant. That is recruiting for eternity, recruiting within the realm of the Christian faith.

As I have mentioned throughout this book, the church and the Fellowship of Christian Athletes have had a profound influence on my life. It was at a Fellowship of Christian Athletes camp that I came to know Christ and became a player on the Christian team.

At Vanderbilt we had a fine Fellowship of Christian Athletes group, led by Frank Hart Smith—we call him "Pogo." Pogo, whom I have known since my college days, was the sponsor and organizer of the FCA at Vandy. When I came to Vanderbilt in 1973 and heard that Pogo was working with FCA, it thrilled me. I could have asked for nothing more satisfying.

Several of the coaches were in the FCA, too, and attended the meetings. This always helps to keep the group moving forward.

Pogo is an unusual guy. I wish every reader could meet him. Pogo is a deep person with creative and unusual ideas. I feel like part of our success as a football team was attributable to him. Pogo not only introduced the guys to Christ, he helped them to grasp the meaning of a real in-depth relationship with the Lord.

While I was at Vanderbilt several of the players accepted Christ as a result of FCA and the influence of Pogo Smith. This group was a vital part of our team.

These fellows were not making these decisions in a "cliqueish" manner. They were doing nothing to bother the team concept of the players, either. There was nothing pious and "holier than thou" about them. I saw many lives changed at Vanderbilt—a lot of people were responsible . . . but above all else it was Pogo Smith . . .

. . . and Bo Patton, who probably started the ball rolling. Bo was a senior during my first year there. Bo really had an impact. I missed him when he was gone. Bo witnessed to several players, including Jamie O'Rourke, our outstanding running back.

Sometimes the Lord has to depend on one man to recruit and stand in the gap. Bo was that man. God had a definite plan for him at Vanderbilt. When one man is willing to be used by God, great things begin to happen.

Now, not every person is called to recruit in exactly the same manner. No two coaches approach the task 100% alike in reaching football players. There is a misconception that every Christian should witness alike—with no variations. That's not right.

God uses different people in different ways for his glory and for his kingdom. A person should ask to be used however God sees fit.

It is unfortunate when we try to fit people into a certain matrix. The other day I met a rodeo clown. He goes to nearly all of these rodeos out West, and he uses his clowning as an entree for the Lord. He gave a tremendous testimony. He is an exceptional soul-winner. He left this message with me: put yourself at God's disposal, and he will use you to his glory and honor.

Every person cannot preach. Every person *can witness* as the Lord leads him. There are quiet witnesses. Not every person is a Paul or Peter. There are vibrant witnesses who have a flair for impressing people and gaining their attention.

But one of the best approaches—you have heard it a thousand times, but I am repeating it—to witnessing is the life you live. I admit that's not all there is, but that's a huge hunk of it. You have been aware of the old adage,

"What you are doing speaks so loud that I can't hear what you're saying!"

The best way some people can witness is *to be*—and also to *be themselves*. There are many places where your Christian life can shine through. God summons us to be who we are and what we are for him.

I'll never forget my experiences with the FCA at Daytona Beach, Florida, during Holy Week in 1966. Many athletes and entertainers were involved. This was a unique situation, and everyone doesn't feel comfortable in that type of setting. I remember discussing this with Raymond Berry, great receiver for the Baltimore Colts several years ago. He said that he didn't feel comfortable, at that time, in that kind of witnessing.

Another thought to carry with you is: God doesn't call us to be successful—he calls us to be faithful. Adoniram Judson worked with the Burmese people for seven years before he baptized his first convert. He must have felt crushed. And yet all the while he exulted, "The future is as bright as the promises of God."

Your approach to witnessing is crucial. There is nothing that turns me off more than to see a person witnessing "in the flesh" and without humility. And there is nothing more obnoxious than for a person to be "goody goody" and full of piousity.

It also bothers me to hear a guy blurt out, "Hey, I've got another soul here," as though the person were a hunk of meat. That guy is telegraphing, "I'm on an ego trip. It bolsters my ego to hunt heads. I'm hanging another scalp on my belt!"

Jesus was the epitome of humility. Can you imagine him coming back to the disciples and blaring out, "Hey, fellows, I really put it to them. Down at Nain a bunch of people came forward. Why, I even raised that widow's son from the dead—my, my, wasn't that something? Man, it was all because of my dynamic preaching. And listen to this—all the people I laid my hands on were healed."? You know the answer to that one.

A witness who honors Christ is wrapped in humility. I am not referring to this put-on humility, either. Oh, I'm so worthless. I'm no count. Now, it may be that God is using a few people who are a little less than humble. If so, it's a-OK with me. But humility is far more useable by the Lord. After all, "To God be the glory. Great things he hath done!"

Witnessing, recruiting for Christ, ought to come naturally. Rather, it ought to come supernaturally. Live in such a manner that you touch the lives of people, and as you do, you have an opportunity to recruit them.

Open yourself to God's will. Pray, "Lord, use me today." Now, if you believe God and trust him to handle the situation, he'll make opportunities for you. And you'd better not pray, "Lord, use me," unless you mean business. Because the Lord will do precisely that.

Throw yourself wide open to God, and he'll amaze you with what he can do in you and through you. *God is ready to use people who are ready to be used.*

The same rules that apply to enlisting football players are true regarding witnessing and sharing your faith. Be tactful. Be friendly. Be persuasive. Be gently forceful. Be sold on what you are selling. Sell yourself but not egotistically. Sell the greatest head coach of all—Christ. Sell the prospect on His university—the church. Stay in touch. Never turn off a prospective person or his family. Emphasize Christ and his strong points—not the weaknesses of persons or churches with which you do not agree.

When we are recruited into God's team, the Holy Spirit indwells our lives. He gives us power to live for God. As a result of his entry, we have certain characteristics or qualities which Paul referred to as "fruit of the Spirit."

But the fruit of the Spirit is love, joy, peace, longsuffering, gentleness, goodness, faith, Meekness, temperance: against such there is no law.[1]

There is no stand-in for the fruit of the Spirit in you. The Spirit can witness through you, even if you are too shy to talk. You can set an example. You can use good language. You can rule out bad habits that are harmful to your body. But, above all else, you can accentuate the positives of Christianity—the "do's" more than the "don't's."

I don't like to major on the "don't's." If you spend enough time working on the "do's," you won't have to worry too much about the negatives. And the fruit of the Spirit are pivotal. The fruit are planted in your life when you receive Christ, but it's up to you to cultivate them.

You can become a more effective recruiter by not depending on "crutches" that help to momentarily bolster your emotions—whether those crutches are alcohol or drugs or what have you.

People are looking for in-depth commitment in the Christian. Paul was dead serious when he testified, "So if eating meat offered to idols is going to make my brother sin, I'll not eat it as long as I live." [2]

All around you there are prospects for the winning team, a team that will lose a few skirmishes down here, but win the ultimate victory throughout eternity. You and I are the Lord's recruiting staff. Are we abiding by the prerequisites for His recruiting?

Commit yourself as a recruiter. Make sure you are in the right spiritual condition. Totally dedicate yourself to the enterprise. You can witness, no matter your background or circumstances.

And trust the greatest head coach of all to set up your contacts. After all, Jesus was the best talent scout and recruiter of all times.

---

1. Galatians 5:22-23
2. 1 Corinthians 8:13

10 Everybody Can't Be an All American

God and man have been awfully good to me. I have never really believed that I have deserved all of the honors and opportunities I have received. I mean it.

In high school I was fortunate enough to be on teams with good players; therefore, I received recognition on all-star teams. I came along at a good time at Bradley Central High School, Cleveland, Tennessee. Being recognized as a high school All-American football player was both a surprise and a tremendous thrill.

In college at Alabama I experienced much the same situation, as I was surrounded by some great players and many good players with extraordinary effort. This enabled me again to receive recognition on some All-American teams.

In high school and college, I was always goal-oriented. I never thought in terms of trying for high awards and honors. Oh, nearly every player envisions himself as being considered the best. Without some of that inspiration, he'll never amount to much.

Yet, the best thing a player can do is to contribute to the team. Every player should realize that he is a part of the team. The rest of the guys enable you to win the honors. They block, they snap the ball, they defend against the offense of the opposing teams, they force fumbles and turnovers from the opposition. Have you ever considered that if a team didn't have a defense, it wouldn't have an offense, because its offense would never get its hands on the ball?

Of course, there are honor and pleasure in special awards. But every person has different abilities. Everybody can't be a football player. In fact, everybody doesn't even want to be a football player.

All the time I talk with players who wanted to get scholarships, but they didn't. They wanted to come to school. Ever since childhood, they've wanted to become an All American. They have wanted to play football with various teams across America. They have always wanted to shine, but couldn't, because they might not have possessed the ability.

There is an apparent frustration, too, in that many young people are forced into certain directions. Maybe dad was a football player, or either a would-be one, and he wants to have vicarious thrills through his son. Or a mother wanted to become an actress, so she pushes her daughter onto the stage.

Believe it or not, there are a few people playing football somewhere who would rather not. But they have pressure from dad who yells, "That's my boy!" On the other hand, there is the boy whose dad insists that his son be a doctor or a lawyer or an oil man.

There is so much wasted talent in America, where people are spending their time and energy in developing things they will never use. Or they do not have abilities in a certain area, yet they persist—and they are square pegs in round holes. I can't imagine me studying opera singing at the Juilliard School of Music. Grand Ole *opera* I might be able to handle.

Every person should find out where his abilities lie—and pursue them for good. Football, after all, is not the end of the world. It's not everything. It's great for some people, but not right for others.

There are many areas in which to study and work. And

all of them—that are moral and legal—are needed. I am not suggesting that a person set his sights on becoming a garbage collector—but what would we do without garbage collectors? Remember what happened to many large cities when garbage was not collected for two or three weeks?

Here we return to the worth of the individual. Each individual has gifts and talents. He has something he can do. Everybody can't be All American or All Conference, when there are thousands of players in the nation and hundreds in the conference.

But every person can do the best he can in his own chosen field. I never judge coaches by their won-loss record. I'm sure that thousands of people do. But there are so many variables. One coach has a 5-5 record, but does it with mediocre material, or the team has a rash of injuries. But another coach has an 8-2 record, and is really not doing as well, because he has a healthy team and better personnel.

When I stand before God at the judgment seat of Christ, he will recall if I was open to his will and working in an area for which he called me. All of us should ask, "Am I in line with what my Creator wants from me? If I am, then I don't have to worry about my won-loss record or what people think of me as a coach (or a housewife or a businessman, etc.), because I have endeavored to do my best with what God gave me."

Obviously, as a coach you will absorb a lion's share of criticism. People like you one Saturday. They don't like you the next Saturday. You're brilliant one Saturday. You're stupid the next. You get good letters and bad letters. You live with criticism. You live with praise. And you accept both.

In the long run, the final judge is God. I want to be in line with him and pleasing to him. These other matters do not bother me, if I know I am pleasing him. But when I am not in tune with him, they do bother me.

We always challenge our players—"we don't care if you're on the first team, the second team, or the third team. Do your best for the team, and all of us win together or lose together. Give it all you've got. Then you're being your best self. Whether you are always successful or not, we like you just the same."

People who don't try, though, never become acquainted with the rewards that come from being part of a team. We want maximum effort from our players. In connection with their effort, we praise players if they do well. Of course, if they are not doing well, we are not able to praise them. Insincere praise is hollow. If we realize that a guy is "busting his gut," no matter how inefficient he may be, we still try to commend him.

When a player does poorly, you have to decide what to do with him and how to motivate him. We make a point of praising a player if he is worthy of praise. There is nothing that can motivate a guy like genuine praise.

We realize that every victory is a team effort. We try to praise the team in general, but if a man is truly outstanding, we usually single him out in front of the whole group. Each coach with his own particular unit goes through the same process. Praise motivation is one of the best types.

People sometimes facetiously remark, "To become famous or rich, you've got to be an athlete or an ex-con." Or, they put these words at the front of that sentence, "To be a well-known Christian. . . ." When I hear that, it makes me wonder if there isn't a hint of jealousy there.

Joe Namath is a guy who has been criticized as much as he has been praised. He is wealthy, young, and handsome. He is the kind of guy who can turn down a four-million-dollar contract without batting an eyelash. But Joe is a likeable person. He is not low or mean. He cares for his parents. He has many good attributes, but the public keys in on what they feel are Joe's weaknesses. I wonder if jealousy is ever involved.

It is not true that you have to become a famous athlete to get somewhere in life. Many a famous athlete has become popular and acclaimed by thousands, only to drop out of sight and end up in oblivion and die in poverty.

And what's wrong with people following athletes or preachers or astronauts or scholars or race car drivers? I see nothing wrong with it, if this identification is kept in proper perspective, and especially if the people I am mentioning have a good reputation.

Americans are still hero worshipers. I would far rather people imitate a clean-living athlete than a hophead freak. Americans admire courage. And strength. We appreciate the person who has ability, ruggedness, and aggressiveness.

But it is far, far better when that hero is a man of convictions and principles. There are still guys who wear "white hats," in spite of the cynics. The Christian's influence is multiplied a thousandfold.

As I have mentioned in another chapter, I have had my heroes. There is Bill Wade who quarterbacked Vanderbilt back in the fifties, and then led the Chicago Bears to the NFL championship in 1963. Bill Wade and others like him intensified my desire to coach and to help motivate young people.

It is marvelous if a person can be in the limelight *for Christ.* Just because a man is an athlete, then, does not imply that he "has it made." After the guy is through college and even the pros, he can't go into a restaurant with a football and buy a meal. He still has to have money, *unless* the restaurant owner is willing to accept the football as security for a bowl of beans and rice.

Very few people are born with a silver spoon in their mouths. Even if they are, at some point in time they have to prove their worth. A person may start out a little higher by being in athletics, but unless he can cut it in the pros and play a long time, he is not going to be fixed financially. He has to make a living even after he plays in the pros.

A man's future is going to depend on how hard he works how dedicated he is, and how committed he is to making a success out of his life.

It is true that a head coach at a major university receives considerable attention in the press. Some coaches are quieter than I am, I guess. Yes, a coach is in a position of influence. I am not going to deny it.

A coach can have a world of influence on young people, not only the one hundred men that make up his total football program, but multitudes of others as well. He is in a position to put in a plug for clean living and high ideals. There are coaches like this all over the country.

The opportunities are myriad to witness to the faith that makes your life turn. In this day, you often hear four-letter words in interviews with athletes, coaches, and managers. But if a coach comes across with clean language and a gracious manner, whether he says a word about his faith, people are going to recognize the difference—that there is something unique about that man. He doesn't need to say: "They played a _____ of a game. He's a _____ ____ player. I'll be _____ if they do." No sir.

To the person who feels he is only average, I would say: "Don't be discouraged. Whether you make All American or All Conference or even make the team, there is a special assignment in life that only you can carry out. There is an exciting venture that the Great Head Coach has for you.

Maybe you've had frustrations. You tried to play ball, and had bad breaks or injuries or failed to fit into the coaching system. Or you had trouble with your home life. You do not feel All American. At times you feel downright miserable and unimportant as a person.

Even though you may feel insignificant, there is an avenue of meaning and fulfillment in your life. Millions of people have found it.

You are worth more than the entire universe. Did you know that? You reply, "Steve, you're crazy!" Yes, you are worth that much. Jesus asked, "For what shall it profit a man, if he shall gain the whole world, and lose his own soul?" [1] One person is worth more than the whole world. The word translated world actually means "all of God's created universe." You are worth more than that.

You can be on God's team. That team is available to all. I am grateful that I am included, and that you are. There is an old hymn which goes, "When the Lord said 'whosoever,' he included me." His team ultimately is the only one that will count.

On his team every person carries equal weight, equal stature, equal importance. God loves us. He cares about us. He wants to be with us. He wants to give us new life. He wants to present us with a new being, a new heart.

And he cares as much about Jack and Susie as he does Steve Sloan. God's love encompasses every person. Now, God has had his called-out servants like David, Moses, Abraham, and Paul. But in a true sense, all of us are "called out"—only comparatively few respond. We can respond and the invitation is open.

To hear Ethel Waters sing "His Eye Is on the Sparrow" sends chills up and down my spine. God sees the fall of the smallest sparrow to the ground. How much more does he care for us. He numbers the hairs of our heads.

All of us—coaches, teachers, parents, businessmen—
ought to feel our worth for one main reason. We are
created in the image of God. Every individual has
dignity and worth before God. If a person can feel
worthwhile, it makes a vast difference. If a person doesn't
feel self-worth, it's hard for him to progress.

I have seen it happen through the years. Here is a person
defeated and stooped down with a complex. God enters
his life, and there is an infusion of grace. The alcoholic
throws away his bottle. The promiscuous person lives clean.
The addict kicks his deadly habit. The gossip cleanses his
tongue. All because they come to know Christ and are
cured. All because they have a genuine, heart-changing
experience. All because they have a "heart transplant."

God does the same for the "good" person, but the person
who has lived his life without an eternal dimension. God
can impart real goodness to the person who has depended
on himself and his own brand of "righteousness."

People become new persons and see life from a different
perspective—in Christ. The change is there when a person
is translated from *existence* to *life*. Some claim that today
is not a day of miracles. I disagree. I run into living,
walking, talking miracles every day. Those people may
not appear on the AP or UPI All-American teams, but
they are all stars, nonetheless.

And let me challenge you. I have had many players
on our teams who were "not good enough," but never
quit. They contributed on the special teams or in practice
or by helping the coaches. But we looked on those guys
as being indispensable to the overall picture—and as being
just as successful as the "All" players. Because those guys
gave all they had.

Those who stick with the task, in spite of the setbacks,
are to be admired more than the guys who have all of

the ability. The non-All Americans made contributions by effort, loyalty, and sweat. Their letters are worth just as much as those earned by All Americans.

When you come down to it, every person—and this is no oversimplification—can be an All American in God's sight.

11 Commitment Is the Key

Commitment is a crucial word. Commitment is extremely important in athletics and life. In football the question is, "How much of himself is a player willing to commit—to lay on the line?"

These days it is far easier to determine a man's commitment because of our use of game films. Ten years ago, film was not nearly as available as it is today. We even film drills, as well as the games. Every day during the season we have an opportunity to review the films of our players. Suppose our lives were filmed that scrupulously?

We can tell which players are taking football seriously— whether a guy is giving us 50 percent or 70 percent or close to 100 percent. It is not difficult for us to judge who is all-out in his commitment.

The question also arises, "How deep is your commitment to your profession of faith?" I study how committed people are to win in life. I remember Paul's unflinching commitment when he declared, "For me to live is Christ, and to die is gain." [1]

How deep do we want to go with our commitment? This is critical. How much do we want to become involved? Dietrich Bonhoeffer was committed enough to die in a Nazi prison camp. John Bunyan testified, "I have loved to hear my Lord spoken of." Bunyan spent twelve years in the Bedford, England, jail. His crime was preaching a free, unfettered gospel. "Whenever I have seen the print of his shoe in the earth," asserted Bunyan, "I have coveted to place mine there, also."

Many people who are not Christians are committed. The Communists are committed. They have pledged themselves to cover the earth with their godless, materialistic philosophy.

Agnostics and atheists are committed. When I was fourteen years old, I traveled to Nashville from Cleveland, Tennessee. Getting to go to the capital was always a special trip. I always liked to visit book stores, and still do. There I read an essay from a book by Robert G. Ingersoll, the famous agnostic and opponent of Christianity. The essay was entitled, "Why I Am Not a Christian."

Later on I read about him and found that he had gone all over the country delivering lectures to disprove the Bible and the Christian faith. In Chicago he held up a Bible and said, "Fifteen years from now, I'll have this book in the morgue." He was committed to an anti-Christian stance.

Fifteen years later he was dead, and the Bible was stronger than ever. There was Voltaire, the French agnostic, who declared: "In a hundred years the Bible will be extinct." In 100 years, long after Voltaire was gone, the Geneva Bible Society purchased his home.

All around us are people who are committed. To me, of course, the greatest example of commitment other than Christ, is the Apostle Paul. At first he was committed to the destruction of Christianity and Christian people. He had his experience with the Lord on the Damascus Road. His direction was reversed. His life changed, and he asserted, "I count all things but loss for the excellency of the knowledge of Christ Jesus my Lord." [2]

And Paul was intent on reaching his people. He testified, "Brethren, my heart's desire and prayer to God for Israel is, that they might be saved." [3]

The Book of Acts, beginning with chapter nine, demonstrates the reversal in Paul's life. In 1 Corinthians Paul speaks of himself as seeing the risen Lord. He calls himself an apostle "born out of due time." [4]

My conviction is that a person can never be his best until he is immersed in whatever he is doing. Commitment spells the distinction between living in the shallows and going out into the depths.

People are confused in their commitments and priorities. They are distracted by the pull of divergent voices.

Once I had a heart-to-heart talk with a coaching friend of mine. He had pressing problems. Guess what he did. He withdrew—he collected himself for a few days and prayed about his dilemmas. He honestly wanted to ascertain the Lord's will in his situation. I was not worried about that coach, because he was going to put it all together—he was going to the right source for help. He recognized that the Lord was with him and would see him through the difficulties and problems.

The prophets of doom are claiming that by the year 2000 A.D., less than two percent of the world's people will be even nominally Christian. It sounds alarming and could happen unless people of faith express commitment to their Lord.

In spite of the gloom, there are many committed Christians left—they are completely committed to walk with Christ every day. But the problem lies with those who are standing on the outer fringes of the faith. They stand on the sidelines and never become involved in the game. They are afraid of getting down to "gut level" Christianity—which involves a deep discipleship. Many of them "joined the church" instead of joining God through Jesus Christ.

Bonhoeffer would call the level of our commitment "cheap grace." From a human standpoint it is easier for us to remain shallow than to go deep. If we stand on the sidelines, we can criticize the other players—and besides, there is no threat of injury.

So many are afraid of sticking their toes into the water for fear they might get wet! While the uncommitted sit around, isms are capturing the world. False cults are multiplying too quickly to keep up with them. These isms and cults have a fanatical following.

Charles Haddon Spurgeon observed, in essence, "If Christian men would only live righteousness with the intensity that evil men live for unrighteousness," what a difference it would make. We are half-hearted and not intense for Christ. Half-hearted players do not win ball games.

> I know you well—you are neither hot nor cold; I wish you
> were one or the other! But since you are merely lukewarm,
> I will spit you out of my mouth! [5]

So many are using the Christian faith as a vehicle for social functions or business instead of a meaningful relationship with God.

Often football players have come into my office and closed the door. They know I am ready and willing to listen. They have asked, "Coach, I'm not doing well in football. How can I do better? I really want to play well." When a guy asks those questions, you simply cannot turn him away without an answer.

If we could sit down together, you might remark, "Steve, I'm not doing well in life. How can I do better? I really want to get in the game.

As best I could, I would try to show you what is available from God himself. God offers you all of the resources of heaven. Why eat from garbage cans when you can have a sirloin strip?

You can have the mind of Christ. You can be filled

up with God himself. You can be changed, different.

Let this mind be in you, which was also in Christ Jesus.[6]

Be not drunk with wine, wherein is excess; but be filled with the Spirit.[7]

In the heart of the Christian faith, there is a depth that causes life to blossom. You can know God in a real way. You may go to church on Sunday, return home, and forget all about it. But when you commit yourself, church and worship and prayer have a new air about them. And when you plunge deeper with God, every day and in every experience and in every way you can learn to love people. You can learn to care about people. You can learn to be your best self.

Avail yourself of God's availability. To the nominal Christian who has wandered away, stop where you are. It's not necessary for us to split theological hairs. Some Christians believe that you can never lose your salvation. Others believe that you can. We're not arguing over that here. Regardless of your circumstances, ask God to assume control of your life. Tell him you want a renewed experience with him. Ask him to deliver you from the shallows and the commonplace. Call it conversation or call it prayer, but talk to him. And you don't have to be careful how you phrase it.

Sometimes a player never realizes where he stands until he watches those game films. Those films don't lie. That's also why instant replay on television can be embarrassing both to players and to officials. Isaiah had no films available, but far better, he had a vision of the Lord. As he prayed in the temple, he "saw the Lord high and lifted up." As he did, Isaiah was struck with his own condition, "Lord, I am a man of unclean lips, and I dwell in the midst of a people of unclean lips; for mine eyes have seen the King, the Lord of hosts." [8]

When Isaiah had an experience with God, he saw not only God—but he saw himself. See yourself through God's eyes. Pray to the Lord, "No matter how it hurts, I want to see myself as I am, and I want to see myself as I could be."

When we have committed ourselves, we cannot rest on our laurels. We cannot lean back and enjoy God's benefits without expecting to move out for him. One year a man can be coach of the year, but if he tries to ride on his laurels, he and his team could plummet. Quit talking about what God did for you years ago. What is he doing through you now—and what are you doing for him? Today. Now. Stop dwelling on yesterday. What does God mean to you today, this very moment?

The children of Israel, when they were in the desert, had to gather the manna, the heavenly food, every day. Unless they did, it rotted and smelled and was fit for nothing. Keep your commitment fresh day by day.

Our Master taught:

Take up the cross, and follow me. [9]

No man, having put his hand to the plough, and looking back, is fit for the kingdom of God. [10]

Paul testified:

I die daily. [11]

I am crucified with Christ: nevertheless I live; yet not I, but Christ liveth in me . . . [12]

Jesus and Paul knew what it was to commit themselves—to love, to serve, and to suffer.

There can be no commitment without commitment to a specific aim, goal, object, or person. The uncommitted person drifts. His allegiance wavers, or he has no allegiance at all. The Christian should be committed to glorifying and honoring his Lord.

Keith Miller in *A Second Touch* describes what I have in mind:

> As our conversations continued, I began to see something I had not noticed at first about the boys' performances during games. One of the devices which the coach employed regularly was the use of game movies for training purposes. On Monday the whole squad, including the coaches, would come in and go over the movies, seeing the good and the bad plays. In talking to some of the players, I had realized the almost fanatical sense of loyalty and respect many of these boys had for their coach. As I watched the replay of some of the films, I saw that these boys did not seem to be playing the game primarily to the audience in the grandstand. They had a reputation for jumping up after being tackled, running back into the huddle, snapping out, and hitting hard with another play. When the excitement of the game mounted and the crowd grew frantic (the other team often becoming rattled), these boys worked like parts of a well oiled machine. One day as I watched the game, I understood how this could be. Although the crowd might not know if each boy executed his specific assignment well, the coach would know. Their cool operation would be seen on Monday even if the press had missed it. I thought, *these boys are unconsciously playing the game to a different audience and it has freed them from the franticness of the crowd!* [13]

Hand in hand with our commitment is the living of that "Full and Meaningful Life." Jesus came that we "might have life and have it more abundantly." [14]

Our immediate goal is to live in the center of God's will. Our long-range goal is to live with the Lord for eternity. When a person has commitment, he sets his eyes on specific goals. He is not content to be just a piece of driftwood.

Throughout this book I am mentioning examples of

commitment and dedication in football players. Most of these overcame insurmountable odds to become star-quality athletes. I am thinking of Rhett Dawson, who was a wide receiver at Florida State when I was offensive coordinator there.

Rhett had undergone surgery on his knee. The doctors also had to remove his spleen, and injuries had forced him out of spring practice my first spring there. But he refused to let adversity dictate his career.

Rhett returned in the fall and finished the year, including the bowl game, with 73 passes caught. He kept working every day after practice. He concentrated. He was an absolutely fearless pass receiver. I believe even if they had tied his hands down, he would have somehow caught the ball.

Rhett didn't have great speed, but his moves were "something else." He is playing Canadian football and doing great.

Commitment was the middle name of Tom Galbierz at Vanderbilt, our nose guard. He is only 5' 10" tall, but he does weigh 215 or 220. Tom was one person who tried to improve on every play. He was never satisfied with anything average. Practice sessions were just as serious as the game.

For years the biggest game on the Vanderbilt schedule has been Tennessee. In 1973 we had an excellent chance to beat them, but lost 20-17 in the final minutes. But Tom was all over the place—his effort was terrific. In 1974 we were leading until the last minute and Tennessee managed a tie by executing a fine two-point conversion. It seems that Tom rose to his heights in those two crucial games with Tennessee.

Commitment is the ingredient that transforms mediocrity into magnificence. Commitment causes people to move beyond the handicaps, hard knocks, and minuses of life. They turn the deficits into surpluses.

Sometimes handicaps can bring out the best in people. Beethoven wrote most of his great symphonies when he was deaf, including his Fifth and Ninth Symphonies. Fanny J. Crosby was blind, and yet over 500 of her hymns are in our hymnals today. John Bunyan wrote the immortal *Pilgrim's Progress* when he was in jail. John Milton wrote *Paradise Lost* and most of his major work when he was blind.

Brian Sternburg, once the world's champion pole vaulter, has risen above paralysis to become a radiant person who enriches the lives of hundreds. At the pinnacle of his pole vaulting success, Brian was jumping on a trampoline. He fell wrong and became paralyzed. Although a paraplegic, his influence is stronger than ever.

Handicaps can bring out the worst, too. One man has a leg injury and becomes a cynical old man. Another has a leg injury and becomes one of the most famous writers in literature, Sir Walter Scott.

My philosophy is this—to move beyond success *or* failure. Commitment should spur us to keep moving, pressing forward. Albert Schweitzer, the famous missionary, was an accomplished theologian, musician, and doctor. But he chose to invest his life in a mission station at Lamberene in West Africa. He could have amassed an empire of wealth, if he had desired. But he committed himself to serve suffering humanity. Service for God and man was moving beyond success or failure.

Commitment implies that we stay out on the cutting edge. This does not involve pressing and anxiety if God is with us on the edge.

So many persons have influenced me to be committed. Charlie Shedd, a best-selling author and minister, has challenged me in my commitment. I was with him at two speaking engagements and had the privilege of talking with him. He wrote me a letter and added this benediction: "May God bless you deep in your heart." Dr. Shedd's very presence expresses humanness and warmth, and a life-changing depth of commitment.

How long will we remain empty, hollow, shallow? When will we grasp the excitement of discipleship? Will we stay in the boat through fear, or will we step out on the waves and, in faith, walk to Jesus?

> For I know whom I have believed, and am persuaded that he is able to keep that which I have committed unto him against that day.[15]

---

1. Philippians 1:21
2. Philippians 3:8
3. Romans 10:1
4. 1 Corinthians 15:8
5. Revelation 3:15-16
6. Philippians 2:5
7. Ephesians 5:18
8. Isaiah 6:5
9. Mark 10:21
10. Luke 9:62
11. 1 Corinthians 15:31
12. Galatians 2:20
13. Keith Miller, *A Second Touch* (Waco: Word Books, 1967), pp. 26-27. Used by permission.
14. John 10:10
15. 2 Timothy 1:12

12 Home Is Where the Heart Is

These days you hear all kinds of alarming statistics about the breakdown and disintegration of the American home. Sometimes you have the impression that certain "professionals" gloat over the dilemma. Figures are quoted to illustrate the peril of the social structures of our nation.

In our country we do have some serious problems with marriage. The divorce rate is extremely high. Why do these problems exist, and what can we do about them?

Before Brenda and I were married, we discussed some of these problems, but of course we weren't aware of all the possibilities of problems in a marriage. Hopefully, some of the experiences we have shared might help another couple.

In our marriage ceremony which was conducted by Loren Young and David Walker, we included excerpts from *The Prophet* by Kahlil Gibran. There is a beauty and mystique about his writing. To me this writing is excellent advice about marriage.

> You were born together, and together you shall be forevermore.
> You shall be together when the white wings of death scatter your days.
> Aye, you shall be together even in the silent memory of God.
> But let there be spaces in your togetherness.
> And let the winds of the heavens dance between you.
>
> Love one another, but make not a bond of love:
> Let it rather be a moving sea between the shores of your souls.

Fill each other's cup but drink not from one cup.
Give one another of your bread but eat not from the same loaf.
Sing and dance together and be joyous, but let each one of you be alone.
Even as the strings of the lute are alone though they quiver with the same music.

Give your hearts, but not into each other's keeping.
For only the hand of Life can contain your hearts.
And stand together yet not too near together:
For the pillars of the temple stand apart,
And the oak tree and the cypress grow not in each other's shadow.[1]

One passage of Scripture in the service was from the Book of Ruth. It is the heartfelt pledge of allegiance from Ruth to Naomi:

Intreat me not to leave thee, or to return from following after thee: for whither thou goest, I will go; and where thou lodgest, I will lodge: thy people shall be my people, and thy God my God.[2]

Before our marriage Brenda and I had an understanding. We had discussed the pressures of my being a coach. We candidly considered the time involvement in my career—the involvement for long periods of time in meetings, practice sessions, recruiting, and all the ramifications of the task.

Also, I was having more speaking engagements than one man could handle. At this writing I have had over 500 of them and they keep coming in, although I am not able to oblige more than a few. I have spoken in churches, at banquets, camps, high schools, colleges, civic clubs, ad infinitum.

I feel very strongly that an understanding of vocations is important before two people get married. If both parties don't thoroughly understand the ambitions of each other, then, in my opinion, they would be better off not married.

Since our marriage we have tried to learn and to grow together. Certainly one's love can mature and deepen. I also feel that we should work at marriage so it can become all God intends it to be.

Brenda and I are, by no means, authorities. We are strictly "lay persons" when it comes to marriage counseling. But we feel that God has helped us to have a marriage based on His will. One of the paradoxes of marriage is how to "become one" and still maintain your own identity. It was and is important to Brenda that I be myself, and that she not try to change everything about me. And I have always wanted Brenda to be herself, except in one or two weak moments.

In many marriages there is almost an immediate campaign to change one another. "Now that we're married, and I have you, why don't you do this and do that and do the other?" Perhaps it is not that verbal, but that precise attitude exists.

Married couples must learn to accept one another in marriage. Funny, they seemed to accept one another *before* marriage. Trying to completely overhaul one another is almost confessing that you have made a drastic mistake to begin with.

Brenda and I, though we would keep our personhood, would be one in God. There is the only "triangle" that should exist—a love triangle involving husband, wife, and God. God has to be included as the unseen guest in the home.

Through the centuries the misconception has abounded—husband and wife must lose identity, especially the wife, and become submerged into one another. That may sound good on paper, but it hardly works in practical life. Each must have a life, of course, a life always considering the other. You still should influence people, and meet people, and relate to people.

We have wanted to become our best selves in marriage, but also to have room for friends and outside activities. As Gibran expresses it: "But let there be space in your togetherness."

Have you ever thought about how little things in football can make the difference? One slip on the Astroturf can make the difference between a loss of yardage and a possible touchdown. One properly-executed play could become the deciding factor between the conference title and a close second. One blocked field goal could decide whether a team finishes in the Top Ten, or maybe eleventh, twelfth, or lower.

There was a song back in the fifties, "Little Things Mean a Lot." And they do. The little card when the Mrs. does not expect it. The candy. The flowers. The note pinned to her house coat. The surprise night out on the town. The little kiss and the little "I love you"—totally without "warning." The considerations, the selflessness of husband and wife toward one another. All of these make the marriage move beyond the humdrum and the "ho hum." They help you to surpass the norm.

Every marriage must have its "never's." We have "never's" for quarterbacks. Charlie Shedd, one of my favorite authors, has touched on a number of "never's" in his books for young men, *Letters to Philip* and *Promises to Peter.*

One "never" I have always emphasized with players who are getting married is: *never criticize your wife in public* or in front of others. And it's probably a good idea not to criticize her at home. A man who criticizes his wife in front of others is asking for serious problems.

Don't even criticize your wife in jest. We never—and

I mean *never*—criticize our quarterbacks in the presence of the team. Those critiques are done in private. This is a grand precept in marriage. And ladies, it applies to you in relation to that man you married, no matter the situation. This criticism bit works in two directions.

Now the positive. *Compliment each other.* A person who is never complimented is like a flower that is never watered. With no praise and appreciation, a person wilts and dies. He may be alive physically, but he dies within the spirit without approval and recognition. Appreciate one another. Express your thanks for one another. Do little things that will enhance your marriage.

There are some things, too, that you have to overlook in one another—the pet peeves, the gripes, the little "burrs" that work themselves under the saddle. Like leaving your shoes in the den, like squeezing the toothpaste tube in the middle, like forgetting to put out the cat, like hanging your trousers on the door knob, like . . .

I could list a thousand pet peeves that people have. If you want to have absolute misery in your marriage, major on the "nit picking." Pick one another to pieces. After a while, you will be driven to these alternatives—separation or divorce, clam up or quit speaking to one another, pull a disappearing act, commit suicide, kill your partner either physically or emotionally, or simply continue living in hell on earth. Those are shoddy alternatives.

Many players, players' wives, and players' girl friends have talked with me about love, courtship, and marriage. I have found that many of the young men do not understand the depth of love that is essential to the woman. Often, they have looked upon their wives as "one of the guys," a "frat brother." And not as a lifetime companion, which is what you will have in marriage.

Many men are not aware a woman wants to be told,

"I love you!" Don't take it for granted. You need to tell her, and tell her often—like several times a day.

And give your mate first priority. Be more considerate. Praise your spouse, even in the presence of your parents. Show your mom and dad that your mate rates first place. This applies to husbands and wives.

When a young couple comes to me, there are a few thoughts I like to share with them.

I deal with how important it is to understand one another. That is the heart of continuing to deepen in marriage. I impress on them the necessity of understanding one another's needs. I advise them to put one another first—first in all relationships. I suggest that instead of asking, "What is important to me?" that they ask, "What is important to my mate?" That removes selfishness in marriage.

Yes, and I would touch on the subject of sex. How can you avoid it? Once again, put the other person first. So many people are sexually incompatible because they think of their own pleasure and satisfaction. They ask, "How can I be satisfied?" instead of answering the question, "How can my mate be satisfied and find fulfillment?"

To those who are about to enter marriage, I would suggest: continue a courtship. You dated before marriage—why not date now? Call your wife from the office and ask her for a date. Use all of the courtesy and politeness that you would when you first asked her for a date.

Continue all the "goodies" you had going before marriage. Although you do not have to be elaborate about it, go out together at least once a week. Eat out. Or drive somewhere—just the two of you—and talk.

It is not difficult for a marriage to "get into a rut." Wives become tired. Husbands become lazy. Work at having time together without the kids, without relatives, without distractions. And concentrate on one another.

Isn't it pathetic that many husbands and wives treat their friends better than they do their mates?

Brenda and I have two fine boys, Clay and Jonathan, which we are very thankful for. Rearing children is an awesome responsibility. Prospective parents should recognize all of the obligations involved. They should, first of all, want children. There is nothing sadder than an unwanted child. There are matters of finance, schooling, care—you name them.

Because of our uncertain, mobile society, children must have all of the love we can give them. Often men are guilty of thinking "maleness" means not showing physical affection for your children, especially if they are boys. One of the greatest gifts a father can give his son is to tell him, "I love you."

To me the pulsebeat of raising children is closeness and warmth. Pick them up. Cuddle them. Snuggle them. When they begin to understand words, they should learn "mamma" and "dadda." But they also should learn "love" and then "I love you." And they can learn from you as you tell them, "I love you, little one."

Even a rough father, when his child falls down and hurts himself, ought to pick the child up and hug him and tell him, "I love you. It's going to be all right." Sad, we have gone away from this affection and closeness and expression of love.

We have moved away from, "I love you. I need you. You're a good boy. You're doing well." And many of us are neglecting our children. We are busy. We are crowded in our schedules. Often the children suffer.

Too, we fail to discipline and to discipline *in love.* Here I am not launching into a lecture about the causes of juvenile delinquency. But every person must have a sense of direction and purpose, especially easily-led youngsters. We must have consistency in disciplining our children. Suppose I warn Clay, "Clay, if you do that again, I'm going to punish you." Clay tests his daddy. He goes right ahead and does it. There is no response from daddy. Clay is not only confused, but he is about to "let the gap down." His young mind begins to put two and two together. "Daddy doesn't mean what he says. Daddy won't do anything to me, no matter what I do."

In another chapter I mention the imperative of enforcing rules for the football team—and being consistent in the carrying out of those rules. This also applies to the rearing of children. Make sure, though, that your rules are Christian and reasonable. If they are Christian, then they will be reasonable.

Can you see the chain reaction that occurs when a child realizes that you are not saying what you mean nor meaning what you say?

We can still teach our children respect for parents, for country, for delegated authority. We can discipline consistently and in love. We can attend church with our children. Go with them. Do not send them or put them out. Be there with them in church.

Discipline with love. Teach them respect. Rear them "in the nurture and admonition of the Lord."

In our family we consider ourselves a team. Clay and Jonathan understand our team effort. We talk about playing on the team together. "Clay, Jonathan is your brother. You are together. You are a team." This sinks into young minds. All of us must do our part. We work together and play together.

All of us in the family try to do as many activities together as possible. We play together, swim together, ride together, eat out together, attend church together. This is vital for the boys, even though they are young and don't understand many things.

There are times, though, that the parents must breathe a sigh of relief. Energetic little children can run you up the wall. This is why it is important to have some time away from the children, either together or separately.

Yes, "home is where the heart is." May God guide your heart in love.

---

1. Reprinted from THE PROPHET, by Kahlil Gibran, with permission of the publisher, Alfred A. Knopf, Inc. Copyright 1923 by Kahlil Gibran; renewal copyright 1951 by Administrators C. T. A. of Kahlil Gibran Estate, and Mary G. Gibran.

2. Ruth 1:16

13 Full of Joy

The story goes that a grandfather carried his grandson for a walk in the country. They came upon the saddest-looking, long-faced mule you can imagine. The mule looked like he had lost his last friend, if in fact mules have friends.

"Granddad," the little boy inquired. "Yes, son, what is it?" the granddad answered.

"Granddad, does that mule have religion?"

"Why, son, why do you ask?"

And the reply came, " 'Cause he's got such a long face!"

Away with that mistaken idea of religion or life. There are so many false concepts around—that your religion has to be a burden, that it is a one-day-a-week affair, that it is divorced from all practical life, that it is for the old, the weak, and the children only, and that religion is the opiate of the people.

The reason people embrace these ideas is that they have looked at faulty exponents of religion. If religion is seen as a dead, dry, dull routine, and if all religion does is make you miserable, and if it gives you nothing to smile about, and nothing to have joy over . . . I can understand why people reject it.

But life is short in this so-called "vale of tears."

Life is too fleeting to consume my time with a wrinkled brow, as though I were on my last leg. Some people, I am afraid, believe in God, but look and act as though he were dead. Many have concluded that God is dead because they have not seen him alive in us.

This is a strange paradox. People want happiness and release from their tensions, so they watch Bob Hope or a Dean Martin "Roast," but when it comes to religion, they think a fellow must conduct himself as if he is presiding over a wake.

The clutch, the regulator, the generator of life resides in a man's ability to laugh and to have a sense of humor. That's what keeps you from losing your temper all the time. That's what keeps you from becoming emotionally ill. Your sense of humor is what causes you to tick and prevents you from flying apart at the seams. Humor can help you to maintain stability.

Jesus was called a man of sorrows and acquainted with grief. But he entered the world to give his disciples joy.

> These things have I spoken unto you, that my joy might remain in you, and that your joy might be full.[1]

> These things have I spoken unto you, that in me ye might have peace. In the world ye shall have tribulation: but be of good cheer: I have overcome the world.[2]

> Hitherto have ye asked nothing in my name: ask and ye shall receive, that your joy may be full.[3]

It is hard to imagine a Christian who does not have joy, and yet I believe that many of them are missing the experiences God has for them. How can a person keep from being joyful about what God has done for us and in us and through us?

The word "joy" appears around 200 times in the Bible. That should spur us to joy in life. Jesus died on the cross and suffered, so we could have joy. He has given us a reason for joy and, yes, the justification for laughter, in spite of life's hard knocks.

If you do not have joy, examine yourself. If Christ does not give you joy, watch out. The heart of the Christian faith is joy because of all that God has accomplished for us. Christ did not mean for his people to live without humor, without joy. He came that we might have life, and that we "might have it more abundantly." [4]

In the will of God there is joy. The Psalmist exulted, "In thy presence there is fulness of joy; at thy right hand there are pleasures for evermore." [5]

In the chapter on "Friendly Persuasion," I speak about many people who have influenced my life. I believe that the most joyful person I have ever seen was not a preacher—at least not an ordained one. That person is my friend, Mrs. Watt in Atlanta. I have never seen such superabundant joy and zest for living. And her joy is infectious.

David Lee at Vanderbilt, our starting quarterback most of 1974, bubbles with Christian joy. Harmon Staus at Texas Tech has a radiance about him. Harmon has plenty of electricity in his faith—a "high" for God. He had a dramatic conversion experience, I believe. David and Harmon are only two of many players who have exemplified a joy inexpressible.

There are church members who seem to feel that a person without God can have as much joy as a person *with*. The fact is—the uncommitted person never has joy. He can have *happiness*, and there is a vast difference between joy and happiness. My feelings at this point do not lord it over those who are not Christians.

From the original language of the New Testament, you learn that *joy* comes from the same root word as *grace*. Grace is the unmerited favor of God within our lives. Joy is in Christ, and only those in God can obtain it. People can have happiness, because happiness depends on what *happens*—our circumstances, our environments, our feelings. But the Christian can have this abiding joy, regardless of what happens to him. Paul and Silas, you remember, were in jail at Philippi. They had been beaten and scourged. They were in chains and the stocks. Yet, they "sang praises to God at midnight."

Of course, all good things come from God. He makes the rain fall on all of us. He showers his blessings on all, the godly and the ungodly, the man of faith and the man of unbelief.

Real joy that touches you down deep proceeds from God. Nothing human can generate it. When a person learns to give, and love, and share Christ, though, there is an experience that supercedes mere happiness. This joy comes from being, feeling, hoping, loving, and sharing.

In the words of little Pippa, in *Pippa Passes* by Robert Browning, "God's in his heaven, and all's right with the world." Insofar as she was concerned, that was absolute truth. When Christ is in our hearts, we can make that statement. In spite of circumstances, it is well with our souls. Because we are straight with God.

A person can have a measure of happiness away from God, but it is shallow and not abiding. It goes up and down according to whim and fancy. You can have joy in Christ, even when your body is racked with pain. Even when you are about to die, or feel that you are going to die.

Payne Best, an Englishman who spent time in a Nazi prison camp, wrote about Dietrich Bonhoeffer, a martyr of the Christian faith. "Bonhoeffer . . . was all humility and sweetness, he always seemed to me to diffuse an atmosphere of happiness, of joy in every smallest detail of life, and of deep gratitude for the mere fact that he was alive . . . He was one of the very few men that I have ever met to whom his God was real and close to him." [6]

Best related how the Nazi agents came for Bonhoeffer and led him away to his death on the gallows. Bonhoeffer said, "This is the end. For me the beginning of life." [7]

Lieutenant Commander Ralph C. Gaither, Jr., spent seven years and four months in North Vietnamese prison camps. It was a miracle he survived. He relates his true story in *With God in a P. O. W. Camp.*

At one point in his imprisonment, he was in a tiny cell which was pitch black for about fourteen hours a day. He could hardly move around in the dark, damp cubicle. He had rats, vermin, and lizards for his company.

I wanted a Christmas tree. The camp, what little we could see, was overgrown with vegetation, but we were not allowed to go anywhere near the growth; were not allowed to bring a stick even the size of a match into the room. Nothing was allowed into our cells, and the frequent searches made sure the barrenness. Outside, we were not even allowed to make a bending motion as though we might pick up something from the ground. That Christmas tree came to mean to me just the opposite of all I was experiencing . . . the season the tree represents spoke of God. I dreamed of a Christmas tree, and the melancholy knowledge that I should be at home settled over me in a pall. I prayed. Then one afternoon after washing my dishes, I turned to take one step back into my cell. I looked down, and on the threshold of my door was a tiny leaf blown by the wind. I picked it up with my toes and carried it inside. . . . I carefully took the leaf from between my toes and looked at it for a long time. I held it to my nose. The perfume of freedom raced up my nostrils, and infused my mind with its power. I fondled the leaf. It was real. I held it in my hand. God had not forgotten me. I set the leaf on the little ledge by the window. Its greenness stood out in stark contrast to the dull, gray bars. Tears rolled down my cheeks. God had given me a Christmas tree. [8]

Even under those conditions, Gaither was thankful because he had the joy of the Lord.

Our joy should include praises to God and thanksgiving. People are afraid of rejoicing for fear that they will be called fanatics. We ought to thank God for every good and perfect gift. We take too many things for granted, and we are not fully appreciative. One of Paul's expressions ends: "And be ye thankful." [9]

In everything we should indicate our joy. And thank God for the opportunity of living in the United States. Because of the Lord, we can "rejoice with joy unspeakable and full of glory." [10]

As you evaluate people, you will find that a thankful person is usually a joyful person.

---

1. John 15:11
2. John 16:33
3. John 16:24
4. John 10:10
5. Psalm 16:11
6. Payne Best, *The Venlo Incident,* p. 180. Cited in Dietrich Bonhoeffer, *Prisoner for God,* Eberhard Bethge, ed. (New York: The Macmillan Company, 1953), pp. 11-12.
7. *Ibid.*
8. Ralph Gaither, *With God in a P. O. W. Camp* (Nashville: Broadman Press, 1973), pp. 30-31.
9. Colossians 3:15
10. 1 Peter 1:8

14 Time on Your Hands

Matthew Arnold called time "a daily miracle."

While we have time, all of us have the same amount of it. Sixty seconds to a minute, sixty minutes to an hour, twenty-four hours in a day, 168 hours in a week, 365 days in a year (one extra in leap year)—or 31,449,600 seconds a year.

"What a difference a day makes, twenty-four little hours," the song went. While time is passing it may seem slow. When it is behind us, we remark, "I wonder where it went. Time flies." Time is a gift from God, and wise use of it keeps our lives in balance.

Jesus was busy "about his Father's business." He had a crowded schedule, but he recognized the value of getting away for meditation, prayer, and rest. Christ had people with him nearly every moment. People pressed around him and made demands on him. Yet, he took the time to withdraw and be by himself.

Why did he go? How could he leave his duties? Thousands of people were clamoring for his healing power, his strength, and his ministry. Jesus had to "refill his cup." There is a lesson in his divine life for every person, no matter how busy he is.

If Jesus were with us in physical presence today, as he was in the first century, he might retreat to the mountains this weekend. Because I am a golf "bug," I'd like to think he might play a round or two of golf.

Jesus realized that it was God's time, and he had to use that time to the optimum advantage. When we are in tune with the will of God, we will acknowledge time as *God's time*, and we will respect it. When we live in an awareness of our stewardship, we will make time count, instead of counting time.

We should have a balance in our use of time. "All work and no play makes Jack a dull boy." All play and no work make him dull, too.

We ought to have an orderly arrangement of time—time with the family, the job, the church, our leisure, and time alone by ourselves. Let me underline it—the secret to proper use of time is to remember that it belongs to God. Live one day at a time. There is nothing wrong with planning, but no matter how you plan, you really can only live one day at a time.

Redd Harper wrote, "I'm following Jesus one step at a time. I live for the moment in his love sublime." The good use of today makes for a better tomorrow. Redd continued, "My spirit grows stronger, each moment, each day. I'm following Jesus each step of the way."

The writer of Ecclesiastes observed, "There is a right time for everything." [1]

During the football season I am flooded with demands and requests. And there is late summer and early fall practice and spring practice and recruiting and doing detail work in my office. We in coaching have to adjust to cramped schedules. Brenda is mighty understanding about my schedule. We have to plan our time, or we face frustration, trouble, and exhaustion. We endeavor to dedicate our time. You have to set aside leisure time, but you must not squander it.

Nearly every day I receive one or more requests to appear somewhere, usually to deliver a speech. Many people become upset if you turn them down. But you can't help it. You cannot please everybody, so you have to please

God first, your family second, and others last. You have to have time for your family, for your faith, and for refreshment. You have to seize your leisure, and you have to schedule time to study and learn and grow as a person.

Call me one-sided, but I had to cast aside nearly every leisure activity but one—golf. I eliminated basketball, baseball, softball, hunting, fishing, boating. I am not recommending this for you. To each his own. I chose one outside outlet—golf—basically because I enjoy it more than anything else.

I enjoy the game. It is a supreme challenge. Where it makes some people nervous, it relaxes me. Brenda knows where to find me. I'll be out on the course. I won't be twenty miles upstream in a canoe. I'll be three miles back in the rough.

You will have to arrange your priorities. I have no idea how some fellows keep up with so many activities—golf, hunting, pistol range, bowling, tennis, backgammon, and 1,001 other diversions.

Do all you can with your family—spend plenty of time with your kids. Dedicate time for witnessing on behalf of your Savior. Let God show you what to do. As I emphasized in the chapter on the home, a man must make time for his wife, and a wife for her husband. They should constantly express love and kindness and thoughtfulness. They should go places and do things together.

The family can attend church *together*. You can arrange to eat as many meals as possible *together* at home. Brenda works it out so we can have breakfast together, unless I am on the road. We have the blessing together. As a family we enjoy going to places like "Prairie Dog Town" or "Opryland U.S.A."—or swimming together in the summer.

A family that can never eat meals as a unit or attend church together is not a togetherness family, for sure. I'm not against television, of course. I have my own television show. But unwise viewing habits can harm a family.

Years ago families used to sit around together and play games or read in the same room. Now, mom and dad watch television—about half the time dad falls asleep unless Raquel Welch is on the tube. The teenagers go off somewhere. The younger children have a TV in their rooms, in many cases.

Four different sets in the house and four different people separated, and not having close communication, can chisel away at family harmony. In the early days of TV such was seldom the case, because most people had only one set. So, the use of the TV set(s) should be decided wisely.

In Nashville I played golf with the coaches. I still do. One of my favorite partners in Nashville was Lou Conner, a lawyer. Lou is an excellent player, and an even better partner. At Alabama I played with Jim Goostree, the trainer for the football team. Jim is not only proficient at golf, he's a devoted Christian. From August to February I seldom play golf, because there simply is not time.

Golf is a marvelous outlet for me. As far as exercise is concerned, I think tennis is better. If I were going to play a game for the sheer exercise, along with fun, I would probably play tennis, handball, or racquet ball. There is quickness involved in those. But I don't play golf for the exercise. I play it for the fun and challenge. For physical exercise I work out at the gym or health spa.

If I went out and played golf and kept thinking about my coaching, I would quit golf, because I play to get away from my daily pressures. I have known people who had neither hobbies nor recreation. They were obsessed with their work, and they carried it home with them. To me that would be killing. I don't know how people survive without some release from business pressures.

I don't think they will ever conquer golf, even though certain players are coming closer. It is not unusual for golfers to shoot 61, 62, or 63 on a par 70 or 72 hole. It is happening more and more. All of the giants of the golf game—Jack Nicklaus, Arnold Palmer, Gary Player, Johnny Miller, and others—will have hot streaks and then take their "lumps." Golf is a many-faceted pursuit. The mental side of the game intrigues me. I like golf's strategy. What club to use on a particular shot. How to play a hole with a "dogleg," how to hit out of a sand trap or from behind a tree. (I've had a lot of practice at those tree shots.)

If recreation is constructive it is worthwhile, provided it is not too time-consuming, doesn't take a person away from his family too much, and doesn't harm anyone. A hobby is a fine diversion. Every person must have a change of pace. It's better to be versatile with your leisure.

If a man has an occupation and he wants to branch out from his occupation for a hobby, I see nothing wrong with it. If a person is a writer, and he wants to write for his hobby, it's OK—but he should perhaps write different types of pieces from his work. If he has done serious writing for a living, why not experiment with comedy or satire?

Now, varied tastes in literature, music, and the arts have helped to round out the Sloans' lives. I appreciate good music, although I have no talent for music at all, I am afraid. I sing in the shower fairly well.

When I was a college senior, I began to create a "hankering" for country and Western music—c & w, they call it. To me many of these songs relate a story. I listen to the words. Part of them amuse me, and others touch my heart.

To me there is considerable honesty and sincerity in many country songs. I listen to country on the radio at home and in the car. We have a collection of records, too. I pick my music, of course, but I like most country and western. It is relaxing to me, and I have respect for those who have musical talent.

It was a delight to be at Vanderbilt in "Music City U.S.A." There I had the opportunity of meeting many stars of the music industry. I guess that Jerry Reed was and is one of Vanderbilt's biggest boosters. He is an all-'round fan—baseball, football, and basketball. I think he was real close to Larry Schmittou, the head recruiter and baseball coach at Vanderbilt. Jerry's a fun person. I admire his talent—he's a comedian, a song writer, a fantastic guitar picker. Jerry is a total performer. He played for a couple of our recruiting dinners and gave the Vanderbilt athletic program some national publicity on talk shows.

Bill Anderson, famous song writer and singer, helped our football program tremendously. He brought his entire band, "The Po' Boys," and played for our prospects at one of our dinners. Bobby Goldsboro sang at one of these dinners, too.

Jerry Reed even attended the Peach Bowl with us. You would have thought he was one of the players. He was in the dressing room, out there on the sidelines with us, with us at halftime, and after the game.

Ralph Emery, whose name is synonymous with country D. J.'ing, gave us loads of publicity on his late-night radio program, and on his other radio and TV programs as well. From Ralph, people all over this land—from New England to Florida to the West Coast—heard about the Vanderbilt Commodores. Ralph attended our recruiting dinners and was always available. Ray Stevens, also a great composer, singer, and musician, played for us to assist with reaching players. I will always be grateful to these men, because they gave freely and willingly of their effort, time, and talent.

Ray Price, who used to call himself "The Cherokee Cowboy," is a smooth singer. His rendition of "Danny Boy" is one of my favorites. And I never grow tired of hearing Eddie Arnold, now in the Country Music Hall of Fame, singing "Cattle Call."

I often remark to myself, "This song that just came out is the greatest. There is nothing to top it." In a few weeks another one comes along and I have the same impression of it. It is hard for me to name my favorite country songs and artists.

By now I hope that I haven't turned off you rock fans or opera buffs or "big band" enthusiasts. Every person has to "have his own things." I like other types of music, also. To hear a band play patriotic music gives me a sense of pride. "The Star Spangled Banner" is always an inspiration to me.

I have mentioned golf and country music. I dearly love to read at home. I am usually going through several books at a time. I read some early in the morning, but usually later on at night. Then, Brenda and I often read at home after Jonathan and Clay have gone to bed.

Many books have molded me as a person. I have already mentioned several in other chapters. One book that has influenced me is *Scottish Chiefs* by Jane Porter. The hero is Sir William Wallace, a man of courage and valor. We cound stand more men of courage and valor.

Andrew Jackson, "Old Hickory," is one of my heroes. Guess where I learned about *Scottish Chiefs?* The local librarian? No. Andrew Jackson recommended the book in one of the volumes I read about him. I gravitate to historical works—both history and fictionalized history.

I am a fan of Hannibal, the Carthaginian general, who fought against the Romans in the Punic Wars. I am impressed by Alexander the Great of Macedon, who con-

quered most of the known world in his day. I have tried
to keep up with military strategists through the years.

Francis Bacon noted that "reading maketh the man."
That is true of me. TV is enjoyable. The right kinds of
movies are entertaining. But a person is missing out unless
he becomes acquainted with the classics of literature. On
the printed page you have access to the supreme ideas
and motivations of the ages. *The Art of Living* by Wilfred
A. Peterson, *The Greatest Salesman in the World* by Og
Mandino, *A Second Touch* by Keith Miller, and *The
Prophet* by Kahlil Gibran are among my favorites.

Miller's *A Second Touch* is initially drawn from the
passage in Mark 8:23-25, where Jesus touched a blind
man's eyes. Jesus asked the man if he could see. The man
replied, "I can see people, but they look like trees walking
around." So Jesus gave a second touch to the man's eyes—
and then he saw men as Christ saw them.[2]

Through my life I have believed, but I have not always
seen clearly and deeply enough into the Christian faith.
I have felt like the blind man who was partially healed.
"Then he saw men as Christ saw them." I want to be
able to see them and to love them as Christ saw them
and loved them.

The Greatest Salesman in the World, a little book, has
big ideas, such as: "Greet each day with love in your heart."
"Persist until you succeed." "I'm nature's greatest miracle."
All of the little book is relevant to me.[3]

The Bible, the Book of books, has opened the eyes of
my understanding. Other books, too, have drawn me nearer
to God's expectations for my life. Since my reading of
A Second Touch, nearly all of my talks have centered
around depth in discipleship.

You can use time, or time can use you. Time can become
your friend or your enemy, according to how you respond.

Live life to the brim. One day the last buzzer will sound. Henry Wadsworth Longfellow wrote:

> What is time?—The shadow on the dial, the striking of the clock, the running of the sand, day and night, summer and winter, months, years, centuries—these are but the arbitrary and outward signs—the measure of time, not time itself. Time is the life of the soul.

---

1. Ecclesiastes 3:1, TLB
2. Miller, *op. cit.*, pp. 6-7.
3. Og Mandino, *The Greatest Salesman in the World* (New York: Magnet Books, 1972).

15 Talking to The Coach

WILL I BE GOOD ENOUGH?

Tonight, Lord, sleep won't come. I can't turn my mind off of football. It's already absorbing all my thoughts, and we don't report in for two more weeks.

I'm getting so nervous, and worrying myself sick about it. I've been running and lifting weights all summer. I really feel good, and I guess I'm in the best shape I've ever been in, *but is it good enough?* There are so many really great players on the team this year.

If I make first string again, or even second string, am I good enough to contribute to the team, really good enough to help us win? Everybody expects so much from me, Lord, and I feel so inadequate! I know my own short-comings better than anybody! I'm so up-tight, because I don't want to let folks down.

I know I could use more speed—there never is too much of that. I know I'll need to study my playbook harder this year, and with my tough schedule, I'm worried about not having enough time for either. See, Lord! How can I possibly go to sleep when I'm tied up in knots, and I know it's going to get worse each day 'til we report in?

Lord, I need to go to sleep right now. Oh, how I need to go to sleep! Please, Lord, tell me what to do to relax.

Don't worry about anything; instead, pray about every-thing; tell God your needs and don't forget to thank him for his answers. If you do this, you will experience God's peace, which is far more wonderful than the human mind

can understand. His peace will keep your thoughts and your hearts quiet and at rest as you trust in Christ Jesus.
Philippians 4:6-7, TLB

I NEVER THOUGHT I'D BE A QUITTER

I'm so fed up tonight, Lord, that I'm thinking of quitting! Yes, me! Can you believe that? Neither can I! The guy . . . who lived to play football, ready to throw in the towel and call it quits. I never thought I'd be a quitter, Lord, but I never knew I'd feel like I do tonight.

I guess the price is more than I'm willing to pay; the pressure is too great; there are too many frustrations. I'm not used to watching from the sidelines. I want to be in the game, Lord, all sixty minutes of the game! I scrimmage hard all week.

To tell the truth, Lord, I guess that's one of the main problems. My replacement showed up in August in better condition, and is still in better shape. Though he's as tired as I am, he still moves quicker. He's got the position nailed down, I know, so I feel like I may as well hang it up.

Nobody could blame me for quitting if another guy's beat me out—permanently—could they, Lord? I've always been first string, and it's embarrassing! Besides, I'm just not sure I'm willing to give the extra effort to win my position back. Lord, I'm so down tonight, the lowest I've ever been since I first realized that football was my game. Would I be letting my coaches and the team down, if I quit? Would you be disappointed in me, Lord? Would I be disappointed in myself?

We are pressed on every side by troubles, but not crushed and broken. We are perplexed because we don't know why things happen as they do, but we don't give up and quit. We get knocked down, but we get up again and keep going.
2 Corinthians 4:8-9, TLB

MY HERO WAS ALWAYS THERE
ON SUNDAY MORNING

Lord, it's time to get up if I'm going to make church this morning, and all I want to do is roll over and go back to sleep. I'm so sore, not really hurt, but there's not a place on me that doesn't ache from the game this weekend. It's a good enough excuse not to make myself get up right now, I keep telling myself.

No, I know it's not! I can make it if I really want to. I'll probably go to sleep during the sermon, or at least "tune the minister out."

You know, Lord, I keep remembering when I was a little boy, my football hero was always there on Sunday morning. Sometimes he limped, or had a bandage on his nose, but he always smiled and carried his Bible.

He didn't even know our names, but we sure knew his! None of us would have missed church, because we knew *he'd* be there. He may have fallen asleep or "tuned the minister out," too, but church meant enough to him to drag his tired, aching body there every Sunday. I mean *every Sunday!* He never missed! He put Christ first, and we knew it!

He had such a special influence, not only on our lives, but on our parents, too. Lord, I guess there'll always be things in every church that we can complain about, but you loved it enough to die for it. Help me to do my part, too . . today and always.

He that saith he abideth in him ought himself also so to walk, even as he walked.

1 John 2:6

TWO A DAYS

"Two a days!" Lord, who ever thought up "two a days"?

It must have been some kind of nut that loved to see torture and misery! It's not really that bad, but it's more of a mental strain than I remember from last year.

I wonder if my legs will ever feel like legs again. Tonight, Lord, I'm beginning to wonder if I'm one of the men or one of the boys. I don't know if I can make it to the end of these "two a days." It seems like our first game will never get here. I wonder if I can last. I'm really thankful for every mile I ran this summer, for all the hills and steps I ran up, for every pound of weights I lifted—but Lord, was it enough?

I know the coaches have got to be tough on us now, to condition us for the whole season, but can I last the whole way? Can I just make it tomorrow, Lord, and the day after that, and the day after that?

Please help me to make it, Lord! You gave me a good, sound, healthy body, but tonight I'm not sure I can make it even one more day. I am really not sure I can make it 'til our first game, much less through the season! What can I do to make it, Lord, to make it all the way? It's such a long time, and the road ahead is tough!

> Don't be anxious about tomorrow. God will take care of your tomorrow too. Live one day at a time.
>
> Matthew 6:34, TLB

I'VE BEEN LOAFING AGAIN, COACH

Lord, I've been goofing off again! The last couple of days, I've just been loafing. The coaches haven't said anything about it . . . yet! Maybe they didn't even notice since they've got so much on their minds right now. They expect 100 percent out of me, every day at practice, as well as during the games, because I've always tried to be that kind of player. They count on me for strong leadership! So, maybe they really didn't notice, and don't know I was loafing! But, Lord, I know it! And you know it!

And it's bugging me tonight! I wonder how many others know it. Funny, but it's so easy to ride on your past reputation, isn't it? But sooner or later, it catches up with you—like tonight; nobody has mentioned it to me, but I'm turning myself in—to you!

I started to say, "Don't let me loaf tomorrow, Lord," but—heck—as tired as I am right now, I wish it was time for tomorrow's practice already. I know I'll feel better inside after I have a chance to put in some extra hustle to make up for yesterday and today.

When you're used to giving it all you've got, you feel that you've cheated yourself, if nobody else, when you give average effort. I pray nobody else noticed! I'm not kidding myself by thinking I'm indispensible! I know how many players are just waiting for a chance to take my place, and they might do a better job. I'll try harder tomorrow, Lord, I promise . . . for the team, but mostly for you and me.

> Let everyone be sure that he is doing his very best, for then he will have the personal satisfaction of work well done, and won't need to compare himself with someone else.
>
> Galatians 6:4, TLB

I HAVEN'T GOTTEN IN A GAME

Lord, the season is nearly over, and I haven't gotten in a game yet! I knew there wouldn't be much of a chance for me to play, but I didn't know how hard it would be week after week. From playing both ways the whole game in high school to not playing at all has been a tough adjustment.

I wonder if people even know I'm on the team. They might if they happen to look down the roster and see my name. My number certainly wouldn't mean anything to them, except it's the cleanest uniform on the sideline every game. Lord, it's hard not to get discouraged and even resentful sometimes when you feel like nobody appreciates you or your effort.

I feel like I could play just as well as the guys I'm behind, when I listen to my heart. But when I'm honest with myself and with you, I know they're better than I am. Lord, let me realize that the first string wouldn't be the great team it is, if it weren't for all of us they scrimmage against every day. We give it all we've got to prepare them for their rough opponents, so I guess we do contribute something.

Some of my buddies didn't even make the team, so at least I ought to be thankful that I'm on the team. The substitutes do get an awful lot of experience, though it's pretty rough sometimes. I've learned so much, not only about football, but about people and so many things. I've made some of the greatest friends—friends that will last a lifetime.

You know, Lord, I guess I'm not so bad off after all! When you think about it, I've really gotten a lot in return for my efforts. Lord, please let me remember this the next time I get to feeling sorry for myself, and remind me that my job is to do my best and be ready when my chance comes.

And some of the parts that seem weakest and least important are really the most necessary.
1 Corinthians 12:22, TLB

We can rejoice, too, when we run into problems and trials for we know that they are good for us—they help us learn to be patient. And patience develops strength of character in us and helps us trust God more each time we use it

until finally our hope and faith are strong and steady.
Romans 5:3-4, TLB

COACH, MAKE ME WORTHY

I got a letter from home today that gave me mixed
emotions, Lord. Our family has always been so close that
we've shared everything, the good and the bad. Ever since
we were little, our folks have been completely honest with
us, and it made us appreciate things more. Many times
we've given up something so that one of the others could
have a new dress, or go on a special weekend, or something.
It might have been tough at the time, but giving, that is
a real sacrifice, is always the most special gift.

Well, Lord, there are financial problems again, but
nothing all of us together can't handle. I just worry about
the pressure on my parents, and I'm concerned that I'm
not in a position to help more right now. But the other
emotion I feel tonight, Lord, is gratitude. Gratitude for
my football scholarship; gratitude that you gave me the
ability and helped me over the years to develop these
abilities; gratitude that the coaches thought I was good
enough and gave me the chance; gratitude that this school
is such a fine and respected institution, so that I can become
anything I want to—if I just apply myself.

I wouldn't be getting this education if it weren't for
football. I wouldn't be able to look forward to helping
my parents, really helping ease their finances later, without
this education that football is making possible. COACH,
make me worthy of this scholarship. Make me work hard
enough to earn it, and deserve it, in the eyes of those who
gave it to me. Don't ever let me fail those who believe
in me—especially you, Lord!

Even while we were still there with you we gave you this

rule: "He who does not work shall not eat."
                                        1 Thessalonians 3:10, TLB

Let your roots grow down into him and draw up nourishment from him. See that you go on growing in the Lord, and become strong and vigorous in the truth. Let your lives overflow with joy and thanksgiving for all he has done.
                                        Colossians 2:7, TLB

THANK YOU FOR BEING OUR MASTER COACH

Lord, football is so important to me! Next to you and my family, I guess it's what means most to me in all the world! I know I should put my education before football, and if I had to give up one or the other, I suppose I would be intelligent enough to realize that I need my education to see me through life more than I need the excitement of football.

But, Lord, I'm just being honest with you right now, because you already know my heart. Right now, I'd rather play football than anything! I'm learning so much more, too, than just the game itself! So many of the principles and lessons, the emotional, mental, and physical disciplines and experiences will get me over many rough spots all through my life. The friendships I'm making through working with my teammates will create lasting bonds. The respect I have for my coaches—as I see their dedication, patience, and desire, not only to create a winning team, but to make winners out of each one of us in the Game of Life—is truly an inspiration!

Let me always show and express my gratitude and appreciation in words as well as actions, since that's what being a Champion is all about. Thank you for being the MASTER COACH of us all, and for already having the Championship Game Plan worked out for all our lives, and mine, too, Lord. Let's talk over the plays I don't understand, or am too stubborn to accept, even though I know you're the Greatest Champion that ever lived! I want to play on your team, Lord—always! Please be patient with me! What do you want me to do?

Be still, and know that I am God.

Psalm 46:10

16 The Man

A Whole New Ball Game has touched on different people who have had profound influence on my life. But there is one person who has meant more to me than all of these people—
and that person is Jesus Christ.

Napoleon Bonaparte once observed, "I know men, and Jesus Christ is no man." What did he mean? That Jesus was not a man? Or that Jesus never existed? No, for Napoleon explained that Jesus was a man above men—no mere man. Napoleon, even though mad for power, realized that the most powerful person in the annals of history was and is Jesus Christ of Nazareth.

Years ago I read the book, *The Man Nobody Knows* by Bruce Barton. This book opened the eyes of my understanding because of the way it depicts Christ. It pictures him as a strong man—not weak, as seen in many artistic representations.

All of us have seen those Medieval paintings of Christ which show him as pale, emaciated, meek, sad, mild. They show him as a weakling with a sallow, jaundiced complexion.

But I think Jesus was a strong man, a carpenter who worked with his hands. He walked everywhere in his ministry, except for an occasional boat trip or donkey ride. The only donkey ride recorded was his "Triumphal Entry" into Jerusalem.

As a boy he played in the hills surrounding Nazareth. He probably tussled and wrestled with his playmates. The

Gospel of Luke notices that "Jesus increased in wisdom and stature, and in favour with God and man." [2]

As a grown man, Jesus cleared the Temple of the moneychangers. Many Bible scholars believe that Jesus drove out the moneychangers twice, once at the beginning of his ministry and once near the close. He made a whip of cords, lashed at the changers, turned over their tables, and shouted, "You will not make my Father's house a den of thieves." No puny, shriveled-up fellow could have done that.

Jesus was man of strength, a man of charisma, a man of power.

After he preached in the synagogue at Nazareth, the people wanted to kill him. They pushed him to the edge of a cliff on the outskirts of the town. Without batting an eyelash, Jesus turned and walked right through the middle of them.

Yet, at the same time, Jesus was and is a man of compassion and tenderness. Think about him when he said, "Let the little children come unto me, and forbid them not, for of such is the kingdom of heaven." And when he spoke softly to the woman caught in the act of adultery, "Neither do I condemn thee: go and sin no more." Or when he opened the eyes of the blind and unstopped the ears of the deaf or caused the lame to walk and throw away their beds and crutches.

Maybe it is selfish of me to think of Jesus as a strong, athletic person, because I was an athlete and work in athletics. I have always felt that Jesus would have been a great athlete. To be a carpenter in those days, without all of these modern tools, Jesus had to lift heavy beams and drive huge pegs with insufficient tools. I believe he was tanned by his exposure to the outdoors as he labored with his hands, arms, back, and legs.

I somehow suppose that he would have enjoyed the challenge of competition. When I was playing college football, I never did think of myself as a good tackler on defense. But I believe that Jesus would be able to tackle with the best of them. I have always thought in terms of Christ's strength. He was strong in his physical and spiritual power, strong in his love for people and for God.

Some have interpreted his driving the moneychangers from the Temple as proof of Jesus' losing his temper. That was not it at all. It was an anger associated with judgment and justice. Jesus had the courage to do the right thing, even though it was unpopular with many of the people.

I hope none of us will ever be guilty of giving people the idea that Jesus is puny and less than a man. It's great to conceive of Jesus Christ as God—and he is God incarnate—but one of the greatest compliments he ever received was from Pontius Pilate. Before the multitude screaming for Jesus' blood, Pilate pointed to Jesus and declared, "Behold the man." And what a man!

The Christian does not serve a weak, defeated Christ, but a magnificent man for all times. God in flesh represents the highest commitment and the deepest love.

Why should a person follow this Jesus? The reason I follow him is that he changed my life. Buddha never did change my life. Neither did Socrates, even though he taught marvelous insights. To me, the basic difference between Christianity and other faiths is: God loves and God forgives, as illustrated by the man, Jesus.

As a younger person, I often sang a chorus called, "He Lives." It closes out, "You ask me how I know He lives; He lives within my heart." Nobody can challenge what has happened to your heart and life. One of the greatest proofs of Christ's resurrection power is a transformed life.

Christ gives us a faith to live for—and to die for. I run

out of adjectives when I consider the life that Christ shares with us. Of course, the problem with so many of us is that we claim the faith, but don't always show it. And don't always make it attractive.

With argumentation and logic, you can never prove the existence of God. I have never tried. You cannot compress God into a test tube. You cannot figure out the infinite with the use of finite instruments. You cannot build a case for the supernatural by natural means.

There are so many people who claim they don't know about God and his Son, Jesus Christ. There are very few people who are actually atheists.

But there are many people who simply do not know. They are agnostics. They don't know whether God exists or if Christ is the Lord and Savior. Here is a message for the doubter who does not know, or who is not sure. Jesus himself said: "If any man will do his will, he shall know the doctrine, whether it be of God." [1]

If a person is sincerely searching for the truth, he can find it. You are not going to find *all* of the truth at once, but you can find the *Author* of all truth. But a person must really want to know. If he trifles with truth, and takes it lightly, he'll never know.

> And ye shall seek me, and find me, when ye shall search for me with all your heart. [2]
>
> Seek ye the Lord while he may be found, call ye upon him while he is near. [3]

It's doubtful that God is going to talk with you in an audible voice, although he once did before we had his written revelation, the Bible. He's not going to communicate through a clap of thunder or a bolt of lightning, although he could if he desired.

If you really don't know, but want to, why not say, "God,

if you are out there somewhere, make yourself known to me.'"? And ask, "Give me the assurance, if you are there." That's the first step for the person who is a sincere agnostic.

Then, pick up the Bible which speaks about *The Man*. Read it, even if you feel it is nothing more than a piece of Oriental literature. Read it objectively—not to criticize or find fault. Read it with openness in the hope that it will offer insight.

But for those who claim to know, how is the knowledge translated into life? As I have gone deeper into the Christian faith, I have become intrigued with the thought that Jesus loves everybody just the same. Money. . . popularity . . . prestige . . . none of these matter from the standpoint of Christ's love. And his love is strong enough for all of us. If only we Christians could become involved with this depth of Christ-love. God is telling us through Christ, "Love one another."

Jesus teaches us that we all need to be loved—we all need to be cared about. We all need to feel that we are important. Everyday is important, and one of the greatest gifts we have is *today*.

Jesus teaches us that we are valuable and worthwhile. What you are is important. What you do is important. You're unique. You're different. You're one of God's miracles. Nobody else in the world is exactly like you.

Revel in the thought. Glory in yourself because God can be glorified through you. Stand up for your family and your name. Be grateful for your heritage. If a person has a sense of worth, he has a sense of respect and dignity.

Because Christ believes we are important, we should recognize the importance of others. If there is anything that Jesus preached, it was the value of personhood—so valuable that he died for all persons.

So, we ought to respect persons because they are persons—God made them, Christ died for them. Never do anything that would take away from your personhood or the personhood of others. That's the main reason to stay away from alcohol, drugs, and other crippling devices. They rob you of personhood.

Jesus wants all of us to know what we believe and why we believe it. We need an anchor when the waves become rough. We need something more than sinking sand. God has promised to sustain us through faith. God is bigger than our problems and has all of the resources of heaven at our fingertips.

Then, I believe that *The Man* wants us to have goals in life. Jesus had his—to please the Father and to accomplish his earthly mission.

> To this end was I born, and for this cause came I into the world, that I should bear witness unto the truth.[4]

> For the Son of man is come to seek and to save that which was lost.[5]

> And it came to pass, when the time was come that he should be received up, he stedfastly set his face to go to Jerusalem.[6]

Jesus had an overriding purpose for living. And he completed his course and carried out his purpose.

The Man would challenge us not to give up, not to quit. He would ask us to give of ourselves. Commitment is the axis on which achievement in life turns.

Christ adds dimension, depth, and hope to life. It was William Ernest Henley, in his *Invictus,* who declared:

> I am the master of my fate.
> I am the captain of my soul.

Henley later committed suicide.

The Christian has Christ as his champion. "The Lord is my champion. I will not be afraid." You can be a winner because of Christ. You can see the fulfillment of the miraculous in your life. Jesus is still performing miracles today in the twentieth century. Any person who has an encounter with Christ is a walking miracle.

Christ gives us an air of expectancy. There is a vibrancy about living for him. We should long for an expectant faith. To the extent that we pray for God to move mountains, and we go out there with shovels and tell everybody to evacuate the area!

Keith Miller, in *A Second Touch*, refers to a man who decided that, for the next week, he was going to do everything just like Jesus would do it. So, Monday morning came along. The man got up too late, grabbed a cup of coffee, and headed for the station to catch the commuter train.

As he was running to the station, he ran into a little boy who was carrying a puzzle. He knocked the boy down, and the puzzle was scattered all over the place. As the train was starting to pull away, the man had to make a quick decision—to catch the train and be late for work, or help pick up the little boy and his puzzle. And the man remembered his commitment to imitate Jesus.

He gently helped the boy up. And he began picking up, one by one, the pieces of the boy's puzzle. The little boy turned to him and asked, "Mister, are you Jesus?"

Who do you remind people of? When your name is called, what do people think of your life?

When you are recruited by *The Great Coach*, and put on his uniform, get into the game, and play on his side, it's . . . A WHOLE NEW BALL GAME!

---

1. John 7:1,7
2. Jeremiah 29:13

3. Isaiah 55:6
4. John 18:37
5. Luke 19:10
6. Luke 9:51
7. Miller, *Op. cit.*, pp. 63-64.